THE
IBM
LESSON

THE
IBM
LESSON

The Profitable Art
of Full Employment

D. Quinn Mills

Times BOOKS

To Chad, Gregg, Lisa, and Shirley

ISBN 0-8129-1690-5
Library of Congress Catalog Card No. 87-40593

Designed by Eric Atherton

Manufactured in the United States of America

9 8 7 6 5 4 3 2

First Edition

ACKNOWLEDGMENTS

A book of this nature is the result of the efforts of many people. Lydia desGroseilliers contributed enormously through interviews, data collection, and analysis. Her insights and hard work greatly enhanced this book.

I am deeply indebted to International Business Machines Corporation and many of its people for assistance in preparing this book.

I am grateful to all the IBMers quoted in the book, and to many who were helpful to me but are not mentioned by name in the text.

Clare DiGiovanni and Mark Cannon were critical readers and helped both with suggestions and with the logistics of getting the manuscript prepared. Robert McIndoe of Emerson Investment Management shared his perspective on IBM with me and also made important suggestions for improving the book.

Hugh O'Neill, my editor, provided additional valuable ideas, as did William Leigh of the Leigh Bureau.

I am also grateful to the Research Division of the Harvard Business School for providing support for some of the work.

All errors and omissions that the book contains are, however, my responsibility alone.

CONTENTS

THE
IBM
LESSON

WHEN THE BOTTOM FALLS OUT

Chapter One

We live in a time in which even the strongest corporations can get into economic trouble, and people who thought their jobs were secure can find themselves forced to make wrenching adjustments.

Searching for security in an instable world, most people try to find it in stability and lack of change. But this book shows that exactly the opposite is true. Security is to be found in the willingness to change.

The traditional patterns of how to be successful are being altered for companies because of the new dynamics of their businesses. Many management practices have become outdated; the conventional ways of controlling the business are no longer effective. Adjusting the business in a timely fashion to new realities has become the key test of executive effectiveness.

This is a story about change: about how employees and a large company adapt when their world turns upside down. It is about how individuals go into different careers and what it means to reorient a person's life. It is also a story about morale: how a company works to earn the loyalty of its employees and what it means to the company to have dedicated people. It is a story about IBM.

Throughout the early 1980s IBM was building for rapid growth. By the end of 1985 the company had more than $50 billion in sales worldwide and employed some four hundred thousand people. The corporation was one of the largest in the world; had an exceptionally strong financial position; and dominated one of the world's fastest growing industries. New people were being hired; new factories were being built; and highly productive automation was being installed in the factories. A support structure was being built in the company to service $100 billion in sales by 1990. Between 1980 and 1985 the company had hired over one hundred and thirty-five thousand new people worldwide to replace attrition and increase the total staff. Even though other large companies were getting into business difficulties, many people at IBM seemed convinced that it was immune from major setbacks.

But the world is increasingly competitive, forcing nations and companies to get reorganized. Technologies are changing and bitter struggles are under way for business and jobs. Despite its great size IBM is not insulated from this.

Suddenly in mid-1985 IBM's sales stopped meeting expectations. The company soon found itself with excess production capacity. IBM had too many people; in particular it had thousands in manufacturing jobs for which it had no immediate need. A major business downturn, it was evident, could happen to anyone. To its surprise the company found itself experiencing the sort of distress being felt by other companies.

Essentially four things had gone wrong for IBM at once. During 1983 and 1984 the company had experienced rapidly rising sales. But in retrospect it was clear that these high sales figures were misleading. Up to the early 1980s the company owned a very large number of machines which customers leased. In the early 1980s companies converted their leased computers to ownership. IBM's sales increased, but not because the company was producing and selling more new machines. Instead sales were up because leasors were buying the equipment they had been leasing. When the conversion to ownership slowed, IBM's revenue growth fell off rapidly.

Second, the computer business was getting much more competitive. IBM's competitors were both domestic and foreign, both large and small. No competitor was as large as IBM or participated in virtually the entire range of the computer industry as IBM did, but each competitor specialized in one or more aspects of the industry. Highly effective competitors faced IBM in every branch of its business. To compete, IBM couldn't just be average in each specialty, it had to equal or surpass the best companies in that branch. Since it was sometimes unable to do this, it began to lose sales to competitors.

Third, IBM had been putting more and more people into manufacturing and headquarters operations, foreseeing strong growth in sales. Yet manufacturing did not really need the additional people. For years the American economy had been moving in the direction of fewer people in manufacturing and more people in services. New automated manufacturing technology made possible large increases in output with little or no increase in manufacturing personnel. And marketing was shortchanged, unfortunately, just at the time at which many customers began to want more help from the manufacturer when they bought computers. In the past many customers had bought the latest computer equipment without a clear understanding of how it was to be used. Now customers wanted not hardware but a solution to their business information problems. They wanted a system, not a box. IBM was slow to perceive this shift in customer perspectives. Also, at this crucial juncture IBM lacked the marketing staff to meet customers' new expectations. Despite its large number of people, their distribution was inappropriate. The organization was out of whack.

Finally, for many reasons, including tax law changes in the United States, customers unexpectedly reduced their purchases of computers and other business equipment. A business slowdown hit the entire industry in the United States pretty much all at once. IBM was not the most hard hit, but it was significantly affected.

And so it was that despite its size and wealth IBM found itself in an industry recession with special problems of its own.

When most companies encounter falling sales and redundant people, they dismiss many employees. But IBM does not do this. For decades it has avoided laying people off for lack of work, and has stressed to its employees the company's commitment to full employment. Under adverse conditions in 1985 and 1986 the company and its employees together took actions which made it possible to avoid layoffs.

To reduce costs the company reduced its hiring and took steps to increase attrition through retirement-incentive programs. These efforts reduced the company's worldwide work force by some 16,000, from 405,500 to about 389,000. Also, by reducing overtime and getting people to take vacation they had earned, the company saved in excess of twelve thousand work years.

But still the company had a substantial excess employee population in its manufacturing and administrative functions, especially in the United States. To alleviate the surplus, some 21,500 people changed assignments, a process IBM refers to as redeployment. Some 9,600 persons were redeployed from manufacturing and product development into sales, systems, and engineering. Another 7,600 people left customer support, overhead, or headquarters assignments to go "back to the field," working directly with customers. Finally, 4,000 persons moved to other locations in assignments similar to those they had been doing because the old location or division or subsidiary was closed or had its mission altered.

In 1986 alone, 12,000 people in the United States accepted substantially different assignments. Electrical engineers working in product development became systems engineers assisting in sales efforts; purchasing managers became marketing representatives (i.e., salespersons); secretaries and manufacturing workers became programmers. Thirty-two hundred people left jobs in manufacturing plants and development labs to go into sales, systems engineering, and administrative positions in marketing locations. Another

2,100 left plants and labs to become programmers and take other positions throughout the company. More than 2,000 people left headquarters operations to go to field sales.[1]

This was not the first time IBM had had to make adjustments in a business downturn. But because this time product, technological, industry, and economic down cycles converged, IBM had a more difficult time than before. And because the company had gotten much larger, the actions the company had to take touched more people more quickly than ever before. These reasons make the story especially worth telling.

A Time of Disillusionment   Losing a job is one of the most difficult things that can happen to a person, and it's no longer something that happens only to blue-collar workers. Today in America almost every person stands in danger of being thrown out of work. Even executives who thought themselves part of a management team at their company and believed that they had a secure career now often find themselves out on the street due to a corporate takeover, restructuring, or downsizing.

Between 1979 and 1984 (the most recent data available), some 10.8 million Americans were laid off or dismissed by a company permanently. Among these were 5.1 million persons with more than three years on the job, and 1.7 million with at least ten years on the job.[2]

---

[1]   Richard Bode, "Redeployment: Moving People to Jobs. A Big Job in Itself," *THINK* (published by IBM), no. 2, 1987, pp. 21 and 22.

[2]   Richard B. McKenzie, "The Displaced-Worker Problem: How Large Is It?" Center for the Study of American Business, Washington University, St. Louis, Publication no. 78, May 1987, p. 5. The calculations are based on William J. Gainer, *Dislocated Workers: Extent of Closures, Layoffs, and the Public and Private Response*, Washington, D.C.: U.S. General Accounting Office, 1986.

Studies of psychological stress have shown that losing a job ranks just behind the death of a loved one, discovery of a serious disease, and divorce in its disruptive effect upon a person's mental health. Suicide, crime, depression, and other personal and social ills often follow. Economic hardship is common. Homes are sometimes lost due to inability to meet mortgage payments, medical care may become prohibitively expensive when coverage is no longer provided by a group health insurance plan at work, and other staples such as clothing and food may be difficult to obtain. In addition, people who have been separated from work often lose confidence in themselves and develop bitterness. Those who remain on the job do not suffer the same stress or economic difficulties, but may share the cynicism and resentment which comes from knowing that they are not secure in their jobs.

As the number of layoffs among managers has risen, the same sort of alienation that has long been observed in blue-collar ranks has invaded the executive suite. Managers are asking themselves whether the game is worth it.[3] According to a survey of middle managers, more than 70 percent in 1975–77 had favorable views of their own opportunities for advancement with their companies. An abrupt decline then occurred, until in 1983–85 only 38 percent reported favorable views about advancement. Similarly, less than half of middle managers now say they would pursue the same career if they were starting over.[4] Other surveys show that managers who in the early 1970s gave favorable ratings to their own managers by more than 70 percent now give unfavorable ratings by the same margin. The doubt that now afflicts American middle management was expressed to me

---

[3] Carol Hymowitz, "Stable Cycles of Executive Careers Shattered by Upheaval in Business," *Wall Street Journal*, May 26, 1987, p. 25.

[4] Ibid., from surveys by the Hay Group.

by one manager: "In America today," he said, "companies borrow money to avoid takeovers or to pay greenmail; do any companies borrow to make an investment in their people?"

The American work force at all levels is somewhat disillusioned. Despite high levels of employment in the aggregate, a great many people are concerned about their future, believe that their employers care little or nothing about them as individuals[5], and therefore live in greater insecurity than at any time since the Great Depression of the 1930s.

Many employees, including professionals and executives, now believe that corporate loyalty is as outdated as a moat and a drawbridge. Business is a contract entered into by employees and stockholders of a company in enlightened self-interest. How can an employee be loyal, it is asked, when the company may not be there tomorrow because it may be taken over or get into business trouble, and even long-service employees pushed out on the street. The only persons who can afford to care about a company's long term, the argument goes, are those who own control. Not even managers can afford to care. They know they might be gone tomorrow.[6]

At present the pressure of insecurity on the individual and the society generally is held in check by the large number of two-income families, so that even if one person loses a job, the family still has some support. It is also mitigated by relatively good economic times and ready availability of alternative work for those who lose jobs. Should an economic downturn occur, however, as it is almost certain

---

[5] For data on this matter see D. Quinn Mills, *Not Like Our Parents: How the Baby Boom Generation Is Changing America* (New York: William Morrow, 1987).
[6] See *After the Axe*, the National Film Board of Canada, 1984.

to do at some time, the situation could become very serious quickly.

Is it possible that American top management believes that insecurity motivates performance by employees? Could the layoffs and dismissals of recent times have not just a financial purpose, but one of instilling fear in the labor force as well? Years ago I heard from an aging mason the story of how during the Great Depression he worked for a contractor who at the close of each week would walk along the wall and tell several bricklayers not to report to work the next week, that he was hiring others in their place. His purpose was to remind those who stayed that they could be as easily replaced should they fall into disfavor with him. Has the technique of this long-dead contractor now become a favored approach of most of our corporations? If so, there is reason to believe that it is not having the desired effect.

There is evidence that the insecurity which now pervades the workplace is damaging American business at a time when international competitive pressures are very strong. Senior managers polled by an executive search firm observed that executives are now less willing to make sacrifices for their firms, and 70 percent said that sagging loyalty had worsened already declining productivity.[7]

Recognizing that they are readily dispensable to their employers, employees, including managers, feel much less loyal to the firms for which they work.[8] A work force riddled with insecurity and with sinking morale is far less productive than it could be.

---

[7]   Egon Zehnder International, reported in the *Wall Street Journal*, September 8, 1987, p. 1.
[8]   See, for example, "The End of Corporate Loyalty," *Business Week*, March 1986.

There Is an Alternative to Layoffs   In surveys of the general population done for this book respondents were asked if companies ought to lay off workers. Generally the response was yes, because the American citizen, always willing to be practical, queried, "What choice do they have?"

The fact is that companies do have a choice. If a company wants to build morale by not laying people off, there is an alternative. This book tells how a company can manage its business and its people so that it does not have to lay off, even when business turns down.

For almost fifty years IBM has not had to lay off any employee. Four decades ago, as the story is told in the company, a business unit at Endicott, New York, decided to cut its costs by laying off nine people. When the act was discovered by headquarters, all those who could be contacted and would return to the company were rehired.

IBM is not the only company in America which as a practice does not lay off employees. However, under the economic pressures of recent years the number of companies which pursue full employment has declined.[9] Periodically start-up companies announce no-layoff policies, as did People Express Airlines, for example. But very often start-ups are unable to fulfill their promises. The list of full-employment companies shortens and the insecurity of the American work force during downturns increases.

Although IBM is not the only full-employment company in America, it is the largest and the most visible.

IBM set about to redeploy its work force to better meet the challenge of the business downturn and to reduce its total employment level, all without resorting to a layoff. By 1988 it appeared that the business downturn was

---

[9]   Daniel Forbes, "The No-Layoff Payoff," *Dun's Business Month*, July 1985, pp. 64–66.

slackening, but the process of redeployment and work-force reduction was continuing under its own momentum. The great ship had been turned in its course, and without a sailor having been lost overboard.

People went willingly to new locations and to new careers, some with eager anticipation, some with hesitation, but all recognizing that the company must adapt itself to altered business conditions. Those who left the company did so via retirement or in some few cases resignation, when relocation was not acceptable. And as we shall see, those who left by refusing offers of jobs at other company locations took with them generous severance pay and benefit packages.

In no community in which IBM had a facility were hundreds or thousands of people thrown suddenly out of work and into an often already overcrowded labor market to shift for themselves. Because layoffs are the common practice among American companies when business turns sour, our news media in recent years have been full of layoff announcements. The contrast between what a full-employment company can do to protect its employees and their communities from disruption and what ordinarily happens in America is dramatic. But it doesn't happen just by will or wish; instead it happens by virtue of deep commitment, long preparation, and hard work on the part of both a company and its employees.

Employment Security   It is crucial that a full-employment company's commitment is to the employment security of the individual, not to job security. In today's fast-changing world no person can expect to have job security throughout his or her career. The jobs we do, the skills that we start our careers with, rapidly become outdated. It is a terrible mistake for workers, managers, and unions to pursue job security as an objective, for it is generally unattainable and the cost of trying to attain it is excessive. What ought to be pursued is adaptability. Recognition of this by both the company and its employees is one of the keys to the success of full employment companies in avoiding layoffs.

Today people and companies confront rapid and dramatic changes in our economy. Anyone and any company can find itself in turmoil. But these situations need not be crises that leave people and communities devastated. Instead, change can be an opportunity for challenge and growth—for both a company and the individuals who work for it.

There is much to be learned about people as they experience change. Many have had to start over, to begin new stages in their careers. They have adapted; found new sources of motivation in themselves and their environments; found new ways to apply what was apparently an irrelevant experience; and seized the chance to find more interesting jobs or ones with greater advancement potential.

People are more adaptable than many managers believe. Given an opportunity, they can find challenge and opportunity in change, even when change is driven by adversity.

But there can be a happy ending to economic dislocations only if a company plans and manages in a special way in order to make full employment a reality; and only if its people are reasonably flexible in adjusting themselves to the new economic realities. There can be no full employment without mutuality between a company and its employees.

Hence IBM's experience throws light on many issues about the management of a modern work force. How can people be motivated? Can today's employees be induced to be a mobile work force? How? What are the secrets of getting middle managers to work hard at implementing corporate policies? What are the telltale signs about what the employees in a company are actually doing with their time?

An Ultimate Test of Managerial Skill   The no-layoff practice stands as a severe reproach to other companies and even to many of our unions. To other corporations the full-employment companies show what many companies might be able to do for the employment security of their own people if they worked to improve managers' skills sufficiently. To the unions and to government officials who call for more job security for workers, the full-employment companies make clear how hollow a promise of job security is that does not guarantee employment but only means that the most senior employee will be the last to be laid off.

The management techniques used to provide full employment are applicable to other business purposes and can help improve the performance of a company generally. In virtually every American corporation today managers are struggling with the question of how to keep people motivated and performing. Full employment is part of the answer to that question, but methods of communication, individual recognition, and change of assignment are also important. Full-employment companies utilize each. Maintaining full employment in a business downturn is perhaps the ultimate test of management skill. It is no accident that the full-employment companies in America are among our best-performing enterprises year in and year out.

Many Americans work in companies that provide little diversity in the job, offer few opportunities for learning and growth, and show little respect for the individual. In such an environment, how does a person keep himself or herself interested? When the corporation doesn't provide a culture or climate in which you can develop, what can you do? Insights into what a person can try to do for himself or herself are readily found in the story of people who have adapted to a changing world in the full-employment companies.

Why do full-employment companies follow this practice? It is expensive in the short run; it requires much management effort; and it is condemned by some spokespersons for the investment community. Traditional American business doctrine is to get rid of excess employees the minute a business downturn looms, and the sooner the better. The managers of full-employment companies must continually face the displeasure of some investors and the puzzlement of managers in other companies about why they go to such extremes for their employees.

There is always an element of suspense when a full-employment company runs into a major business downturn. Can a layoff be avoided? The deck is stacked against it. Most other companies lay off. Wall Street favors cutbacks. The cost of keeping people on may be prohibitive unless the business can be turned around rapidly. This question was also there for IBM. When business turned down sharply in 1985, could the company preserve full employment?

Full-employment companies believe that they have an obligation to their employees which extends to employment security; they also believe that over the long haul it is good business. "Full employment is the cornerstone of the loyalty of our employees to the company," John Akers, IBM's chairman, commented in a speech at Harvard University early in 1987. With employee loyalty, levels of human performance that other companies only dream about become reality. Employment security and employee loyalty do not protect a company from mistakes in the marketplace, but they help it to prosper over the long term.

Managers in full-employment companies recognize that they are building employee loyalty and helping the business by their efforts to avoid layoffs. But they are also providing employees with change, learning, challenge, and opportunity, and these qualities are as important as employment security itself in building commitment and loyalty in employees.

At the core of the full-employment practice is a different way of thinking about the human being and the organization. Managers in most American companies think as follows: "The company has a job to be done, so I'll hire a person to fill it. If we no longer have the job, the person ought to go."

Managers in full-employment companies think differently, and are sent through intensive training to achieve the difference in perspective. A manager is taught to think: "The company has a group of people. We also have jobs that need to be done now. When the jobs change or are eliminated, we retrain the people to do the new tasks."

Because the companies which utilize full employment are generally profitable, it is tempting to conclude that the full-employment practice is simply a luxury which they have because they can afford it, while other companies cannot. This is a matter which is discussed in depth in Chapter 12. It ought to be said here, however, that none of the full employment companies lack for other things to do with their financial resources than spend them on employment security. On the contrary, new business projects, increases in research and development, and dividends to shareholders are among the competing uses of funds. Also, financially successful companies rarely stay that way over decades by squandering money on luxuries. Instead they are financially successful in part because they carefully husband resources. It is not for lack of other opportunities to spend money, nor because of a taste for luxuries that a few American companies have adopted a no-layoff practice. Rather, these companies believe that full employment is good business.

Exciting Lessons for Management There are exciting lessons for managers in any company in the story of IBM's efforts to preserve full employment. Nor are these lessons limited to how to avoid layoffs. Instead, much of what IBM accomplished involved broadly applicable processes very difficult for any company to put into practice, but from which all would benefit. Here are the most significant:

1. A business slowdown usually means sacrifices. Our story tells how at IBM, business adversity was transformed into personal opportunity, not sacrifice, for employees who were directly affected.

2. Employees ordinarily must be compelled to do what is needed for the business. Here employees did what the corporation needed and saw it as voluntary, rather than compulsory.

3. At many companies a downturn hurts employee morale. In this instance the response to a business difficulty was managed so that the morale of employees was enhanced rather than reduced.

4. When business gets bad, there are many rumors about why and what it will mean. Here the company managed to tell everywhere the same story about what was being done and why, so that each employee understood what was happening to him or her and the reasons for it.

5. Many companies find it very difficult to get middle managers to buy into corporate objectives, especially when a downturn has occurred. At IBM top corporate executives brought all levels of management into alignment with the company's objectives, despite the company's actions sometimes being against individual managers' own interests.

6. Generally, communications refer to what the company tells the people, whether they listen or not. In this instance communication efforts not only informed employees as to what was occurring but also caused them to take actions that helped to attain corporate objectives.

7. Top executives in many organizations try to maintain a distance from the difficulties that affect employees in a downturn. Here top management demonstrated its commitment to the employees by staying deeply involved in the redeployment process.

8. In most businesses, when one part of the business gets in trouble, its people must bear the adverse consequences alone. This story tells how weakness in certain parts of the business (manufacturing and engineering) became a source of opportunity for people in other parts (sales and programming).

This is a story about how a company and its people have found opportunity in business distress by building on their commitment to each other.

Summary of Significant Points

■ Today's managers must handle an increasingly complex set of problems, including a turbulent economy, fierce international competition, new legislation, a rapidly changing marketplace, and an economic base that is shifting from manufacturing to services. In this environment, even a company like IBM, with some of the most sophisticated business and strategic planners in the world, can fail to anticipate a major business downturn.

■ The industrial world's work force from blue-collar workers to executives has entered a time of disillusionment: people are concerned about their future, believe that their employers care little or nothing about them, and therefore live with greater personal insecurity than at any time since the Great Depression. In such an environment the benefits to a company of offering secure employment are greater than ever.

■ Many people are able to accept much greater degrees of change in their lives than they and others think, and find in the experience new sources of vitality in their lives.

■ Fitting the person solely to a job is dead. Modern companies hire a person not just to perform a task but as an individual with adaptive capacity for many jobs. Companies that make this effort to look ahead and prepare for the future have time to react.

■ When a downturn occurs for most companies, a first reaction is to lay off employees. But there are significant losses to a company from this approach, and IBM has demonstrated an alternative and better use of its people.

■ To be successful, every company needs a good working relationship with its employees. IBM more than any other American corporation refuses to let short-term business reverses interfere with its relationship with its employees. Instead, it tries to turn business reverses into career opportunities for individuals and thereby reinforces the connection of its people to the company. This is a modern alchemy through which business difficulty becomes personal opportunity and rebounds to the corporation's gain through enhanced employee commitment.

■ An account of how IBM manages this process provides a rich source of ideas for executives in other companies.

FROM FISH TO FOWL: REMISSIONING BOULDER

Chapter Two

Rumors That the End is Near   Throughout the suburbs north of
Denver rumors were rife that IBM would soon close its manufacturing facility at Boulder, idling several thousand people.
Workers in the plant were very well aware of the softness
throughout the data processing industry, other areas of IBM,
and their own product line—copiers. Those who had been
some years at the plant were aware that it had rarely been
profitable for IBM and that though there had been one brief
period of prosperity, the corporation was again sustaining
losses from Boulder. All about them people saw the evidence
of recession. Storage Technology, the largest employer in the
immediate area and another member of the high-tech industry, had recently entered a bankruptcy reorganization and
most of its work force had lost their jobs. "People had been
given two weeks and ushered out," said Linda Jorgenson,
mayor of Boulder. "There were no advance discussions and
no one was well informed. The impact of the layoffs in the
area had been substantial."

To add to the region's woes, the petroleum
exploration and development industry had collapsed, with
the loss of thousands of additional jobs. Already Colorado's
unemployment rate had climbed to about 10 percent and it
seemed likely that it would rise again should IBM react to its
emerging business slump by laying off people.

Concern about possible layoffs among IBM
employees did not seem unusual to themselves or to their
neighbors and acquaintances. Although the company had not
had a layoff at Boulder, and had not dismissed employees
anywhere for lack of work for many years, people knew that
no company could simply ignore the marketplace. If times
got bad enough, then layoffs were possible, even at IBM. And
the corporation had always qualified its commitment to full
employment by describing the commitment as a practice,
which presumably could be changed, and not as a policy,
which the company insisted it would relinquish not at all.

Other well-known companies had recently abandoned no-layoff policies in much publicized layoffs—including, among others, Storage Technology, Advanced Micro Devices, Apple Computer, and Eastman Kodak Company. Would IBM do the same? A feeling that significant events were about to occur grew in the community. Something was going to happen to the Boulder facility and to the five thousand people who worked there, and through them to their families and the communities in which they lived.

"When IBM came to Boulder," said Linda Jorgenson, "it built an attractive physical plant, car-pooled employees to reduce noise, contributed to child-care facilities, and loaned executives to our community periodically to assist in resolving our problems. We depended on IBM for a great deal. We knew what had happened at Storage Technology, and we knew that IBM was having trouble with its business. If they shut the facility or a large part of it, Boulder would have been devastated. We were all waiting to see what IBM was going to do."

"Where Is Our Property?"—IBM Comes to Boulder   Boulder, Colorado, and its smaller neighbor Longmont are picturesque communities nestled at the foot of the Rocky Mountains. From the plains on which the towns are located snow-covered peaks are visible almost year round. In spring great clouds gather over the mountains and darkened curtains of rain can be seen by residents of the towns who are miles away. On some days winds come down off the mountain peaks at more than a hundred miles per hour, so that asphalt shingles which would blow off a roof in minutes have given way to cedar shakes nailed securely onto housetops. To the north and west lie the dramatically beautiful high peaks and alpine valleys of Rocky Mountain National Park. Herds of elk, or wapiti (to use the Indian designation), wander only yards from the winding highways by which tourists traverse the park. To the

south on the flat, arid prairie east of the mountains lies Denver with its million residents, tall buildings, and vigorous commerce.

Boulder and Longmont are communities to which people become deeply attached. The life-style is casual and outdoors, with a wide variety of recreational opportunities coexisting with apparent ease beside many of the cultural attractions of the large urban area. Shopping malls, bowling alleys, motion picture houses, and fast-food outlets line busy thoroughfares punctuated by traffic lights, yet only a few miles from broad ranchlands and pristine mountain valleys. A person finds more variety offered than most places, and a grandeur of natural surroundings which seems to elevate and enlarge the human spirit.

In the early 1960s IBM selected Boulder as the site for one of the growing company's new facilities, employing much the same criteria the company generally uses to make such choices. For IBM primary consideration in locating a facility include proximity to a university, good elementary and secondary school systems, and the sort of small but not isolated community which provides a desirable environment so that people with the necessary skills can be attracted. In addition, the company pays attention to the sorts of matters more commonly treated in economic analyses of plant location decisions, including labor costs and proximity to markets.

In the Boulder area IBM identified an almost ideal site for a new plant. The main campus of the University of Colorado is in Boulder, a substantial accumulation of buildings in which housing and education is provided to tens of thousands of students. The university engages many educators distinguished in their fields. But except for the large size of the university, Boulder is in all other ways very much a small town—the kind of community in which IBMers can feel secure and comfortable—a good place to bring up children. Denver, close by, offers the amenities of a major metropolitan area, and the mountains a magnificent environment for recreation.

On March 3, 1965, Dick Whalen, the first site manager for IBM Boulder, threw a luncheon to the business executives, bankers, educators, politicians, and press of Colorado to announce IBM's plans for the Boulder facility. Thomas Watson, Jr., and several other high-level corporate officials came from IBM headquarters to the meeting. Tom Watson gave a brief speech, and when he finished, was asked by a reporter, "Mr. Watson, are you going to allow the city of Boulder to annex your property?"

According to Whalen, Tom Watson looked at him and whispered, "I thought our property was in Boulder."

Whalen answered, "Tom, this is the first time I've ever been here. I don't know where it is."

Watson and Whalen both turned to another IBM executive, who shook his head negatively; then to another who said, "I've never seen it either."

Finally Watson turned to the audience and said, "Will somebody out there tell us where our property is?" The audience burst into uproarious laughter.

As it turned out, the property was on the line between two townships, and the buildings of the facility lie partly in Boulder and partly in Longmont.[1]

And so it was that in 1965 the corporation opened a sprawling facility on the gently undulating grassy plains east of Boulder. A complex of rectangular buildings interconnect in a labyrinth of corridors, passageways, and staircases. Externally the buildings are much alike. Each is light in color and rectangular in shape. Inside, some buildings

---

[1]   "Celebrate the Spirit," Information Products Division, IBM, Boulder, Colorado, June 1985, pp. 2–3.

have the mazelike clutter of office units; others the broad open spaces that characterize manufacturing facilities; and still others the hermetically sealed sterility of a computer facility. But a person walking through the facility cannot escape the impression that none of the space is irrevocably committed to its present use. The entire complex gives the impression of a giant concrete-floored, metal-walled box, the interior of which could be converted to virtually any use simply by the removal or relocation of partitions and the installation or downgrading of ventilation systems.

The plant's work force grew rapidly. Some 4,000 people were employed at Boulder by the end of the first eighteen months of operation, 900 of whom were transferred in, the remaining 3,100 had been hired locally. By the 1970s the plant employed some 5,000 people, and there it remained into the mid-1980s.

Today the Boulder plant is readily accessible from the highway by large roads clearly identified as leading to a facility of the IBM corporation. Each building, however, is sealed by extensive security systems which make a casual visit impossible. Once inside, there is greater freedom of movement. Adjacent to a central open space is a light and generously sized cafeteria from whose windows are dramatic views of the distant mountain peaks, and which serves, in IBM fashion, as the primary dining room for all the facility's employees—factory workers as well as programming professionals.

By 1985 about half the work force at Boulder were employed in the manufacturing plant, primarily assembling copiers and printers. The assembly processes were inordinately complex. Some copiers had as many as fifteen thousand separate parts. So complex were many of Boulder's products that they did not lend themselves to the extensive automation installed in recent years in other IBM plants. Wide aisles ran through the manufacturing buildings, which merged into one another imperceptibly. Along the aisles ran small programmable carts which carried parts and completed assemblies. These small robots had largely replaced the forklift trucks which are so common in other warehouses and manufacturing plants, and which still existed at Boulder only in significantly reduced numbers. Workers and visitors quickly got over the impulse to step quickly from the path of the robots, since they were equipped with bumper-type sensors on all sides that caused them to stop immediately when any obstacle was encountered.

When the transportation robots were first introduced to the plant in the early 1980s, they were immediately christened the seven dwarfs and given the names Walt Disney had created for his motion picture. There were now many more than seven of the robots, but the original units could be readily identified by the names printed boldly on their metal framework: Dopey, Sneezy, Doc, Grumpy, and so on.

But despite the presence of the seven dwarfs, the production technology in the Boulder facility was not highly sophisticated. Instead, much more extensive automation had been introduced into two other plants which produced somewhat similar products (and in consequence were organizationally in the same division as Boulder): Lexington, Kentucky, and Charlotte, North Carolina. In part it was the complexity of Boulder's products that limited automation.

Boulder had been started as a plant producing tape drives for computers. In the mid-1970s the production of copiers and copier supplies was moved from Lexington to Boulder. For a number of years the complexity of the copiers had resulted in the production of units which experienced early reliability problems. Consequently, potential customers were reluctant to purchase from the plant, and the economic return on manufacturing at Boulder was insignificant. A major effort to improve the quality of production at Boulder was initiated in the early 1980s, and after a few years attained its purpose. The quality effort had succeeded in part because of its focus not only on direct manufacturing but on the associated services and functions. "If you want to improve morale and efficiency," said Bob Gholson, a manager who played a significant role in the quality effort and whom we shall meet again in a subsequent assignment, "remove the things that frustrate people." Sales and profits from manufacturing at Boulder rose. There was talk of expansion of manufacturing at Boulder if sales growth in the industry continued. The effort to improve the quality of production at Boulder was a positive experience which helped to prepare the people in the facility for the difficulties and challenges which lay ahead.

Unfortunately, as the plant was beginning to achieve its potential, the business equipment industry entered a general economic downturn. Soon excess capacity became evident at many of IBM's manufacturing facilities. In order to cut costs the corporation began to consolidate production activity. Manufacture of floppy disk drives for mini-computers had been introduced at Boulder in 1980, employing some four hundred people. In July 1986, floppy disk production was moved to Lexington.

The downturn in sales continued, and the plant manager in Boulder, as well as his counterparts at Lexington and Charlotte, reported to corporate headquarters that they each possessed substantial excess capacity in plant space, equipment, and staff. In December 1985, the division was told by group headquarters that Boulder needed to be restructured, but it was left to the division to determine how it should be done.

George Corsilia, the site manager at Boulder, formed a small group to decide what missions could be brought into Boulder if manufacturing were moved to fully utilize other IBM factories. In February and March 1986, a task force composed of twelve to fifteen people representing the three plant sites, distribution and business systems management, and people from the business group and corporate level, composing a sort of microcosm of the company, spent six weeks deciding what changes should be made and what impact they would have on people.

"We kept asking ourselves," Corsilia said, " 'What makes sense for the company and what is manageable at the site levels?' We took the plan and made it realistic. We decided who and what would actually move."

Excess capacity at Boulder was evident to many in the facility, and seeing the task forces at work, the rumor mill began to churn out prospects for a shutdown at Boulder. At corporate headquarters in Armonk, New York, the measurements being studied by IBM's top executives showed excess manufacturing capacity and high costs. Top corporate officers began to tell executives of the business group which included Boulder that "you guys have problems."[2] Soon the group's executives responded to the corporate officers with a plan that included the remissioning of Boulder and an expected payback to the company of the costs of the remissioning over five years.

In early March 1986, the top executives at Boulder were informed that its business group and the corporation had approved a plan by which the facility would be retained but its mission would be dramatically altered. Most manufacturing activities were to be moved from Boulder to either the Lexington or Charlotte plants, and Boulder would be remissioned as a programming and service facility. The decision to move manufacturing from Boulder was dictated by the corporation's continuing efforts to cut costs to stay

---

[2]   Frank Metz, Jr., senior vice president, corporate finance and planning staffs, interview.

competitive in a then shrinking market. IBM's employment costs were relatively high compared to those of its competitors, both domestic and foreign, and the corporation had been automating its manufacturing plants extensively in order to cut costs. Extensive automation at Lexington and Charlotte had made those plants more efficient than the Boulder facility, and resulted in the decision to consolidate Boulder production in the other two sites.

Boulder management had played a role in the decision to consolidate by ending production at Boulder, and had been involved to a small degree in the earlier decisions which focused automation in the other plants. But basically, these decisions had been made at the division and group level and approved by the top corporate officers. Nor was this the first time that Boulder had been strongly affected by decisions made at higher levels: the decision to open the Boulder facility, to assign to it the production of tape drives, to alter its assignment from tape drives to copiers, to bring in floppy disk production and then to move it out, had each been a higher-level decision that brought work to Boulder or moved it out.

Carrying Out the Remissioning   Although site-level management had only a minor role in the decisions about what mission Boulder was to have, it had a great deal to do with how the decisions of the division and the corporation were carried out. April 6, 1986, had been designated by the division as the date for the commencement of the formal transition of the facility. Early in March, Boulder management began to communicate the decision to the plant's work force.

So rife had been the expectation that Boulder would be phased out that news of the remissioning was received with relief, both among IBM employees and in the community at large as news of the IBM decision crept out. Boulder would not be cast adrift, another victim of changing economic times, but instead would remain part of the corporation's team, called upon to adapt to the times.

Frank Metz went to Boulder to meet with the facility's top twenty managers about the reasons for the remissioning. He also addressed all managers at the plant, who had been assembled in a theater. Asked why he had personally gone to Boulder, Metz replied, "I was involved in making the decision. I wanted every manager to understand what the rationale was and what the outcome would be. I wanted each manager to understand that he or she shared responsibility for the outcome. And finally, I think that someone like myself at the center of a decision like this should expose himself. If someone makes a decision such as this, he should come out and acknowledge it."

George Corsilia decided to personally convey the message about Boulder's remissioning to the plant's employees. Notification to suppliers and customers of IBM and to the community was made by other members of the facility's management. Specifically, both employees and community leaders were informed that over a period of many months the manufacture of copiers was to cease. Boulder would no longer be a manufacturing plant. But the site would be redirected as a distribution center for all IBM products west of the Mississippi River, and as a programming center for the corporation. Distribution and programming would add as many jobs in the short run as manufacturing would surrender, and in the future the facility might well increase its total employment. As for the manufacturing employees who would be released from their current jobs, some would relocate, some retire, some leave IBM, and the remainder would be retrained for new assignments at Boulder—and each employee would make the choice for himself or herself. To give graphic evidence of the corporation's commitment to maintaining the Boulder facility at roughly its current level of activity, a programming unit involved in defense applications was transferred in total from Westlake, California, to Boulder, and an international procurement group from Poughkeepsie, New York, was also brought to Boulder. With each of these groups came some new employees who relocated to Boulder, but new jobs for existing Boulder employees were also created.

Corsilia recognized that it was not sufficient merely to inform employees that Boulder would be remissioned. Something should be said that would give each employee some sense of what would be in store for him or her. There were some five thousand people in three shifts to whom it was necessary to describe which jobs would be changing and which would remain unchanged in the remissioning. A task force on the remissioning worked closely with communications experts at corporate headquarters to prepare an information program.

Initially Corsilia met with all managers at the site giving them materials about the remissioning. The management group was broken into smaller units to discuss questions raised. The work force as a whole was then broken into groups of four to five hundred and meetings were held by Corsilia with each. After each presentation by the site manager, lower-level managers took their own direct reports aside and discussed the matter. Information was posted on bulletin boards; managers held many one-on-one and small-group meetings. The intent was that each employee would know what was likely to happen to his or her own job and what options he or she would have.

Once decisions had been made and announced about what missions would be transferred into Boulder and which would be moved out, Corsilia established another task force to coordinate the activities. The group worked out a schedule and tried to plan every detail. Meetings were held every Friday. Corsilia said that he spent most of his time refereeing the meetings and saying, "Where's the problem going to be?"

The remissioning of Boulder became one of the largest such efforts ever accomplished by IBM. The movement of manufacturing out of Boulder was an enormous task. Large plastic extruding and shaping machines were loaded onto railway cars or trucks and carried across the nation. More than 10,500 tons of equipment were shipped out, including fourteen plastic presses, each as large as a small locomotive, which were sent to Lexington.

Building areas that had been used for manufacturing were redesigned and adapted for computer use, requiring extensive improvement of the ventilation systems so that the cooler temperatures and cleaner air required by operating large computers could be provided. Open factory floors were converted to offices. Construction crews became common in the plants, crowding and complicating the activities that continued. Colorado's depressed economy ironically facilitated the remissioning because skilled construction mechanics and contractors were readily available to do the refitting.

In eight months the Boulder site was transformed from a manufacturing facility into a major center for distribution, information systems, and programming work for the federal government. Nine new missions moved into Boulder as others left. To accommodate the new missions, temporary space was leased for about 900 employees while construction work was done in the Boulder facility. Nearly 200,000 linear feet of interior walls were taken down, 154 miles of cables installed for systems connections, 17 million feet of wire and cables were added, 140,000 feet of carpeting placed down, 26,250 ceiling tiles placed, 414 doors hung, and three new electrical substations built. More than 2,600 desks were moved in and out and 2,530 telephones added, moved, or changed.

Human Transformation   In mid-February 1986, site management began to work out in detail its personnel guidelines for
the remissioning. As described by Corsilia, the planning followed two basic guidelines:

1. Each person should be given exactly the same reason for
what the company is doing. If that seems impossible, it is
necessary to rethink what is being done. People were to be
told what was happening based on the exact reason why it
was being done.

2. Management was not to wait for people to ask questions.
To assume that people don't ask because they know the answers is naive. Managers would hold frequent meetings and
at every meeting would inform employees about their options.

"My philosophy," Corsilia added, "is to give
employees so much information that they finally tell you to
stop. If employees didn't understand why the company was
making the changes, then they would resist them, and we
would be unable to carry out the remissioning as quickly and
efficiently as we needed to."

On April 22, 1986, Corsilia stood before
groups of 400 to 700 employees and in a series of meetings
explained to all 5,200 employees what was happening at
Boulder. He also talked with all managers five times over the
next eight months to be sure they were completely informed.

The redeployment of employees from phased-
out work to new or ongoing work was not done according
to the merit practices which IBM uses for virtually all other
personnel actions. Ordinarily, better assignments, more rapid
promotion, larger salary increases, and other advantages are
conveyed to employees in IBM on the basis of their performance as evaluated by their managers. But redeployment is
only partly a matter of merit. All employees, regardless of
level of performance, are entitled to new job offers, and managers who are accustomed to differentiating among their sub-

ordinates on the basis of performance are prevented from doing so during a redeployment.

IBM managers are ordinarily free to select the persons they will hire, but during the remissioning they were often restricted to choosing candidates made available from those being displaced. Managers whose operations were being moved to Boulder, as from Westlake, California, and Poughkeepsie, New York, were told that during the remissioning they would not be allowed to play by the ordinary rules of the IBM corporation. Instead, for the transition period, they would be operating to a large degree not on the merit system, but by one based on availability and seniority. Preference for available jobs would go first to the most senior IBM employees displaced by the remissioning. Because this was so dramatic a departure from the norm, there was resistance by some managers, and a special quality of effort was needed to accomplish the redeployment. The person chosen for this task by Corsilia was Bob Gholson, whom we met earlier in a key role in the successful effort to improve the quality of copier production at Boulder.

Gholson came to the job of personnel resource manager at Boulder from an assignment in production. The resource management job was newly created for the remissioning effort, but in a way Bob had been well prepared for it. He had, he said, "made a career in IBM out of not having to pick a career." He had started in accounting with IBM and been through various assignments since, including jobs in production and personnel. He was comfortable with transitions in his own career, and was thereby well suited to help others make transitions themselves.

Immediately Gholson was asked by senior line management to form a task force to work on the redeployment of people. Because the remissioning occurred in stages, the group determined to work with ninety-day "windows."

That is, they would begin to seek alternate employment for each individual no more than ninety days before the scheduled termination of the person's current assignment. To start earlier would threaten to disrupt ongoing production by removing from their positions employees who would still be needed for many months. But personnel management was careful to assure employees who would not be released from manufacturing assignments until later that good positions would not all be gone by the time of their availability. And the task group worked with incoming management to see that that was in fact the case.

While the physical transformation of the plant proceeded, staff and line management labored at the human transformation. All employees at Boulder who would be affected by the remissioning were promised that they would be offered another job with IBM. Many people interviewed for several positions. And with a few exceptions, as we shall see in a moment, the job offers made by the company were at the Boulder facility.

At the outset of remissioning, Boulder employed some 2,700 people in manufacturing activities. Within the first fourteen months after the announcement of the phase-out of manufacturing, approximately 1,800 were displaced. Approximately 639 left the site—some relocated with the manufacturing activities with which they had been associated (including 32 tool and die makers whose tool-building skills the company did not want to lose); some went into marketing as part of a broad corporate effort to place more salespeople in the field; about 200 retired; and only 20 persons chose to take severance pay and leave IBM rather than be retrained or relocated. Approximately 1,200 people changed careers or transferred to new assignments at the Boulder site, of whom roughly 625 were initially blue-collar workers (so-called non-exempts in American terminology) and about 575 were initially technical or professional workers (so-called exempts).

No Disguised Layoff These statistics make it clear that IBM's insistence that it truly has retrained and redeployed much of its work force at Boulder is correct. Sometimes it is alleged that when there is a surplus of employees, a company may offer employees jobs which they cannot do, or relocations which they will not take, so that employees are forced to resign. Forced resignations are of course a form of disguised layoff.

But at Boulder ordinary attrition from the work force averaged about 3 percent per annum, a relatively low figure by the experience of most American corporations, and this figure did not increase as a result of the remissioning. As mentioned above, only twenty people left Boulder by resignation during the first fourteen months of the remissioning, and none by layoff.

For the corporation as a whole during the corporate-wide redeployment effort of 1985–87, the attrition rate did not increase, but rather fell back, despite the increase in early retirements. That is, the attrition rate excluding retirements actually declined during the redeployment effort. A similar situation had been closely monitored by the company in 1971 when there was a substantial redeployment of people from manufacturing and development to sales. The attrition rate in 1971 fell to 2 percent, lower than the rate of the previous and succeeding years. The evidence is a tribute to the company's commitment to retain its employees and to find new and productive assignments which people would accept voluntarily.

The redeployment staff and manufacturing line management did a great deal to be sure that no IBM employee was put into a position in which he or she felt obligated to resign from the corporation as a result of changes brought on by the remissioning. Because Boulder was to continue to be an operating facility, no employee was given the final yes or no choice between geographic relocation or no

IBM job at all. Every person displaced by the remissioning was offered another job at Boulder and the training necessary to qualify for it.

So-called polling was used to move employees out of terminated jobs into new positions. That is, a seniority list was prepared for each group of jobs with related skills, and as new positions opened, displaced or soon-to-be displaced employees were offered the new positions in order of length of service. If the senior employee refused the job, it would pass to the next senior, until the bottom person might have only that job offered to him and therefore have little option except to accept it. Where a job involved a lesser salary grade, the employee would continue to be granted salary increases based on his or her old salary grade for up to two years, during which time the opportunity for transfer or restoration might permit him or her to retain his previous pay grade indefinitely. Fourteen months into the redeployment effort, ten of seventy-eight people who had been downgraded in job level in going into new positions had been able to restore their old level.

People also could be placed in positions in various ways. If a person were continually passed over, he or she was eventually offered a position by agreement in advance between the personnel staff and the managers who had the position. Managers of activities remaining at Boulder or being moved in had an obligation to provide work for redeployed persons.

Some jobs were singled out as not being worthy of a final offer of a job to a displaced employee. One such job was that of security officer because of the unusual schedule of such work, continuing as it does night and day and on holidays. Management feared that an employee offered a job in security might feel compelled to choose between a proper home life and working for IBM, and top management did not want to appear to force people to choose to leave the company in order to be with their families.

It is evident from this description of how IBM management conducted the redeployment of IBM's human resources at Boulder that the company actively sought to retain as many employees as it could.

Redeploying Managers   Not only production, clerical, and technical people were redeployed at Boulder, but managers as well. One manager mentioned going from manufacturing to his new assignment in programming. "Hello," he reported saying to the group he now supervised, "I'm your new manager. Would you please tell me what you do so that I can be of some assistance to you?"

This is a far cry from the concept so prevalent in America of the manager as the boss who knows all about the work and gives the people who report to him detailed direction about how to do their jobs. IBM's conception is of a group of professional employees who know their own jobs and whose manager is the interface between them and others in the corporation so that they are able to perform their work well. The manager is expert in IBM's personnel and other management systems and can learn different aspects of the company's work as he or she receives different assignments. This is held to be the case in all but the most technically complex circumstances.

Fourteen months after the start of the remissioning, two-thirds of the work being done at Boulder is new, and one-eighth of the managers have been redeployed into areas in which they previously had little or no experience. Boulder is in the process of being converted from an Information Products Division manufacturing and development site to one with no manufacturing and considerable placement and distribution activity. It is a site in transition, but not one that is dying. The site population has *increased* approximately 14 percent; its exempt population is up 8 percent; its average age has increased; and its years of service is about the same as before.

In some respects the most surprising aspect of human redeployment at Boulder involves the retraining of five hundred blue-collar production workers for jobs in distribution and programming. In some instances the jobs into which people moved were not startlingly different from those which they left. Distribution facilities, for example, involve numerous jobs much like those in warehousing in a manufacturing plant. Other jobs which former blue-collar workers took were very different, however. In the next chapter we will meet production workers who moved into programming jobs, generally after months of rigorous classroom and on-the-job training. Are people really this adaptable?

Again and again in our interviews I asked IBM managers at Boulder whether or not they had hired people with a view to their ultimate retrainability. Always they said no. People had been hired to meet the needs of the moment in the jobs then vacant. It is true that IBM receives applications for employment from many talented and ambitious people, and presumably IBM managers select the best among the applicants. And it is also true that applicants for work have generally been screened by personnel professionals before being referred for job interviews to managers with vacancies. But these circumstances do not mean that IBM factory workers are any more or less likely than their counterparts in other companies to be reassignable to very different occupations. On average, IBM pays ahead of the local labor market for similar jobs, so that people who are able to command professional salaries are not likely to come to IBM to work as blue-collar employees. Hence even though IBM may have the best of American blue-collar talent, it is still blue-collar, and the redeployment effort is a dramatic statement about the adaptability of which American workers are capable. IBM managers recognize it as such. As Dick Jacquemard, a fourth-level manufacturing manager (there are six levels of management in the facility) at Boulder whose own story in the remissioning will be told in the next chapter, said, "Any worker can be retrained again and again in his or her lifetime for very different assignments."

Summary of Significant Points

■ As our economic base continues to shift from manufacturing to services, managers can make effective use of unnecessary production facilities and avoid layoffs by remissioning sites and redeploying people.

■ By remissioning its facility at Boulder from a manufacturing plant to a state-of-the-art programming and service center, IBM demonstrated that employees can be successfully retrained for new careers on a large scale.

■ Information can be used to combat resistance to change. IBM did so by flooding employees with information, giving each of them the same rationale for the company's actions, and making sure that they understood their options.

■ Commitment by the company to employment security for employees reduces their stress and encourages them to be successful in new assignments.

■ Line management execution of the process, with personnel staff advice and expertise, facilitates a transition because it is clear that the line is responsible for both the problem and the solution.

CLOSING GREENCASTLE

Chapter Three

"If You're Having an Affair . . ." One Sunday morning David Kennedy, the manager of the IBM distribution facility at Greencastle, Indiana, told his wife that he was going to Indianapolis for a meeting. He'd be spending the day at a motel, he added, and wouldn't be back until late Sunday. As he talked, he seemed distracted and concerned. His wife knew that he hadn't been sleeping well lately, and had been cautious and secretive with her, which was out of character for Dave. He'd also been traveling a lot recently. She was angry and hurt, and suddenly blurted out to him, "Dave, you've been acting very strangely lately. If you are fooling around, it's really going to cost you."

Kennedy had not told his wife of the closing of the facility because he did not want her to be compromised by any questions asked of her. A week previously he had been informed by the headquarters of his division that the plant he managed, where more than nine hundred people made their living, was very likely to be shut down. Six days ago he had reviewed the business case that brought the final decision to a close. Four other managers in the facility had also been told, and each one had been asked to sign an agreement with the corporation by which they swore not to reveal the information until a specified date. The date was to be Tuesday, November 11, Veterans Day!

From the moment the team of Greencastle managers had learned of the closing all had been cloak and dagger. They held long meetings in David's office, the door uncharacteristically closed. As the days passed, David noticed that his secretary was watching him quizzically. She knows something is up, he thought, but she doesn't know what.

Joe Taylor had been at Greencastle since it opened. For eighteen years he ran a rotary press making keypunch cards. When Greencastle went from cards to magnetic tapes he became a technician in the ribbon manufacturing area. He put ink on the ribbons, "an interesting operation," he commented, "but a very messy one." He became first shift manager for ribbon manufacturing, and in 1974 took responsibility for all ribbon manufacturing. Then the company moved ribbon manufacturing to Dayton, New Jersey, and after helping with the move, Joe became a personnel specialist. In 1980 he returned to line management running the second- and third-shift distribution operations.

In the fall of 1986 David Kennedy asked Joe to do a report for him. Kennedy told him that it had to be done by early November. But when Joe stopped by to deliver the report, Kennedy's secretary took it and said her boss was too busy for the next several days to discuss it. "I thought that was strange," Taylor said. "Kennedy and four other men were locked up in his office for several days. But I didn't let on that I thought something important was happening."

As the date of announcing the closing approached, David Kennedy and his compatriots became increasingly tense. Minor incidents assumed frightening aspects.

One day an early season snow fell on Greencastle. David had gone into a rest room in the warehouse area of the plant. A warehouse worker was standing next to him. He turned to Kennedy and looking him directly in the eye said, "I hear we're closing the plant."

Kennedy's heart all but stopped. He couldn't believe the word had gotten out. Worse, he knew he would now have to confront his closest associates, the four other managers sworn to secrecy about the closing, and find out which one had betrayed his and the company's trust. Who had let the secret out?

"I've got to call a plant-wide meeting instantly," David told himself. "I can't afford to let rumors start floating—not here, where I've so many friends and we have tried to be so careful; not now, when it's only a few days away from our planned announcement. I have an outline of the speech that's to be given next week, I can use it today."

The warehouse worker stood looking at Kennedy, surprise building in his eyes as the plant manager hesitated longer and longer without replying. Noticing the concern in his eyes, David asked suddenly, "What did you say?"

"I said," the man answered, "that it's snowing pretty hard outside. I heard we might close the plant due to the snow."

Greencastle nestles among the rolling hills of central Indiana about an hour's drive west of Indianapolis. It is a community of about nine thousand people, and is home to a fine liberal arts school, DePauw University. People in this part of the Midwest commonly have jobs in corporate facilities which dot the small towns, and also farm plots of land which they own. They are a hardworking, hospitable people, more contented than competitive, who are removed from much of the bustle of the metropolitan areas but who keep themselves aware of the outside world via television and newsmagazines.

In 1953 IBM established a manufacturing plant at Greencastle—its fifth manufacturing location. (Today the company has twenty-five.) Initially the plant produced the once-ubiquitous IBM punched card, but as card usage declined due to tape- and later disk-driven computers, the plant was converted to tape production. In 1975–76 IBM no longer needed the manufacturing capacity of the Greencastle plant. Not desiring to disrupt the life of the community and its employees, however, and having a growing business, the company decided to remission the facility rather than close it. In consequence, Greencastle was remissioned in the mid-seventies as a distribution center.

In its new role, Greencastle received shipments from suppliers to IBM and warehoused the materials for later shipment to IBM's parts field distribution centers. Similarly, it received products from the manufacturing plants for later shipments to customers. The plant was an intermediate stop. When the remissioning was done, virtually all of Greencastle's manufacturing people were retrained for jobs in the distribution facility.

But by the mid-1980s IBM's business had undergone another major change. Now in increasing competition with other American companies and foreign firms, the company could no longer afford the luxury cost of a bulk holding facility. Instead, inventory management techniques were improved at both IBM's own plants and those of its suppliers, so that the materials and products which had been stored at Greencastle were now kept at the producing plants until shipment was made direct to the users.

In addition, a Japanese concept, so-called just-in-time inventory management, was appropriated by IBM and its suppliers as well as by many other American companies. Instead of the traditional American practice of storing manufactured products so that they would be available whenever a customer needed them—what might be called "just-in-case" inventory management—production is scheduled to be done just prior to when the product is desired by the customer. The result is that the plant can ship directly to the customer without the need for an intermediate warehousing facility like Greencastle. In this manner the management expertise of corporations in Japan came suddenly to impact the jobs of 950 Americans in central Indiana.

The division studied the location of its distribution facilities, but also took a careful look at the demographics of their work forces. Greencastle had an especially long-service employee group (an average of twenty-two years of service to the company). By the fall of 1986, over half the plant's staff was eligible to retire—far more than at other distribution facilities. It followed that the disruption in people's lives was most likely to be minimized should Greencastle be chosen for closure.

People could not, however, simply be instructed to retire. Fortunately, a corporate-wide retirement incentive program was under way and its options were likely to be attractive to those eligible in Greencastle. For those who chose not to retire, the corporation would assure alternate employment at other IBM sites as nearby as possible. When the decision to close had been made, much of the work from Greencastle would be transferred to Mechanicsburg. The most common offers of further employment with IBM would be for jobs there.

Upon receiving notification in early November that Greencastle was to be closed, Kennedy and his four associates sat down in his office for days on end to plan the closing. Among their activities was to take a list of employees, 985 in all, to discuss how each individual would be likely to react to the decision. Who would retire? Who would move? Who would be likely to resign from IBM to stay in the area?

David Kennedy had started his association with the Greencastle facility in 1966, and though he had had assignments elsewhere in the twenty intervening years, he had been at Greencastle long enough, through several stays, that he knew most of the staff personally, and even knew about their family situations. The management team attempted to sort out individuals with special needs so that they could be ready to address their specific concerns.

Although division and corporate executives had made the final decision to close Greencastle, they left to Kennedy and his on-site management team the job of carrying out the closure. Division staffs called periodically to offer assistance, and they prepared the questions and answers to be handed to Greencastle's middle- and first-line management on the day of the announcement. Greencastle managers would have an especially tough job that day. They would have to address the concerns of the rank and file while wondering themselves about what would happen to their own careers and lives.

When was the announcement to be made? and how? Kennedy and his team decided against Friday, November 7, in order not to leave people stewing over the weekend without their managers to whom they could take developing concerns. Monday, November 10, was unacceptable, because all managers would have to be told on Friday to report early Monday morning to be prepared before the general announcement. Friday scheduling of such a meeting, highly unusual, would have started speculation and rumors. Hence, the best way was to tell the managers on Monday to report early Tuesday, and to prepare for a general announcement later Tuesday morning.

At 6:30 A.M. on Tuesday morning all managers reported to the plant and were informed by Charley Biggar, National Service Division president, and Kennedy about the closing. Then all department heads met with their own managers to brief them further from materials handed out by Kennedy. Questions and answers had been prepared for all managers. All workers on second and third shifts had been told to report to the plant at 11:15 A.M. for a meeting, and all first-shift employees were released from their jobs at that hour as well to assemble.

Kennedy also prepared for medical emergencies. Two doctors and two nurses were on hand at the facility should anyone have a medical problem. Since the city officials of Greencastle were also to be informed that day, and the then mayor was known to have a health problem, a nurse was sent with the team who was to inform the mayor.

When Kennedy left his home to go to the plant on that morning he filled his pockets with extra handkerchiefs. "I knew people were going to cry," he said.

"The Toughest Thing I've Ever Done in My Career"   Charley Biggar was the president of the National Service Division of IBM. Greencastle was one of several facilities dedicated to his di-

vision, and Greencastle's almost one thousand people made up less than 5 percent of his division's population. To make the announcement to Greencastle's work force that the plant was to close would be a miserable task. Yet everyone felt it crucial that the division president explain to the Greencastle people what was being done and why. And so at 11:15 A.M. on Tuesday morning, November 11, 1986, Charley stood before all employees of IBM Greencastle in their plant to personally tell them that the facility would be closed. "It was the toughest thing I've ever done in my career," he said later.

Biggar and Kennedy made the announcement speaking from an outline. They explained the difficult economic environment of the company. They detailed the actions which IBM had taken to try to avoid additional steps. Then they announced that IBM would consolidate Greencastle's functions with those of Mechanicsburg and Lexington, and that the transfer of functions from Greencastle would be completed by March 1987. On that date, the Greencastle plant would close.

Every employee would be offered jobs at other IBM locations. All moves would be at IBM's expense. The company would purchase the homes of all who chose to relocate at the pre-announcement appraised value. (Since relocation would soon place more than 10 percent of Greencastle's housing on the market, causing prices to fall dramatically, this was a major benefit.)

For those who chose to leave IBM, the company would provide double separation pay, retraining assistance in the amount of $5,000, assistance in finding another job, and pay for increased travel or commuting costs to the new job for two years. These same benefits were available to those who chose to take the IBM incentive retirement package and retire from the company.

A previous Greencastle site manager, Robert D. Holum, was brought back to Greencastle from his job managing standard products distribution at Mechanicsburg to help employees find jobs, to take matters up the IBM chain of command quickly if Greencastle people felt they weren't being treated right, and to help with any personal hardships. Since Holum knew the Greencastle people, he was well suited for the task.

Kennedy ended his and Biggar's presentation by saying that the decision to close Greencastle was a painful one, but that a great deal of work remained ahead to make the moves successful for both the company and the people, and that he needed the help and support of each person at Greencastle.

As Biggar and Kennedy concluded, the plant's employees, whose faces were shocked and tear-stained, applauded.

"I teach courses in business ethics," said Larry Coleman, professor of business at Indiana State University at Terre Haute. "Late in 1986 I had been asked by a large company to do some training for people they were laying off. The managers in the company didn't want to face the people who were being sent away, so they hired me to do it.

"At the time I was doing that, IBM announced the Greencastle closing. Several of my students came to me and said it would be interesting to contrast what the one company was doing with IBM's approach. So I started looking more closely at the differences between the two corporations.

"When IBM made the announcement about Greencastle, they did it very differently from the company for which I did work. IBM brought in top guns from the division. They wanted to make sure that the employees knew that the company wasn't abandoning them. IBM made it a point to send people personally to talk to the mayor and the lieutenant governor and other officials. Throughout the whole process, IBM put people first.

"Dave Kennedy and Charley Biggar got up in front of the whole plant and explained what was going to be done and how it would affect individuals. IBM believes in keeping its employees informed. They not only say what they're doing, but they say why they are doing it. Many other companies don't explain to their employees the reasons behind their actions. When Kennedy was through, the whole place cheered him because he was so honest and forthright."

"Like a Band-Aid on a Hairy Chest"   "They made the announcement of the closing with everybody there and they did it quick," said Dick Callahan, a fifty-six-year-old skilled worker at Greencastle. "If they hadn't, rumors would have gotten out. At IBM, our rumors are horrible. Within two hours a rumor gets magnified. Within a couple of days the rumor would be like a Band-Aid on a hairy chest—very painful to pull off. They did it quick, so it wouldn't hurt so badly.

"When Biggar made the announcement," Callahan continued, "the women were more emotional—they were crying. It bothered everyone. I felt sorry for Biggar and Kennedy to have to do it. They tried to make it sound as good as they could, but there was no way to make the people feel good, and they knew it."

Ralph Jordan was fifty-five years old and had twenty-nine years with IBM. "It was Veterans Day, and on every Veterans Day in the past we had a moment of silence at the Greencastle plant. But we didn't have one that day. In the warehouse our faces were pretty long. Dave Kennedy's face and Charley Biggar's had no smiles on them. We were all extremely solemn. I can't remember what Dave or Charley said."

Sherry McMains had been with IBM since 1983. "On the morning of November 11 they announced a meeting for the whole plant. Nothing like that had ever happened before. My department had a great sense of humor. Prior to the meeting we all got together and made a list on a board of all the things the meeting could be about. One person suggested that Greencastle was going to be remissioned; and another said that we were going to reduce staff. One person even suggested that the company would shut Greencastle down, but we said that was crazy. They would never shut us down.

"I can't remember what was said at the November 11 meeting," she continued. "The only thing I remember is Charley Biggar saying, 'Therefore, we're closing this site.' His expression and concern was very genuine.

"After the announcement we went to our manager's office to sit down and talk it out with him. We were all in a state of shock. My manager discussed what our options were: we could move with the company; we could retire; or we could resign. I couldn't retire. I tried to call my husband, but I couldn't get an outside line. I was devastated. I was in shock."

Soon after the announcement David Kennedy began a steady stream of interviews about the closing. "I did an interview with a group of high school students representing the high school newspaper. I remember how concerned they were about the whole situation," he said.

Kennedy also met with the media. "I had planned in advance what I would say to them," he commented, "but it was an extremely exhausting ordeal. I think they were looking for what we did wrong. They wanted to publish the bad news."

Late one evening Kennedy received a call from one of the warehouse workers. He said to Kennedy, "Dave, I called because I think right now you need a warm fuzzy [i.e., someone who cares]. I just saw you on TV and you looked terrible. Take care of yourself. We'll be just fine."

"The key to the whole thing was communications," Kennedy said. "People can handle good news, and they can handle bad news. But they can't live with no news."

"The Worst Part Came Afterward"   Difficult as the November 11 meeting was, a staff engineer insisted that "the worst part came afterward."

"Around Christmastime people thought that the company was going to change its mind because the plant seemed to be operating as usual. But by January and February, reality soaked in as equipment began to be moved out. It was a miserable two months. There was no joy in the last couple of months at the Greencastle plant.

"My department was responsible for the move," he continued. "We were one of the big villains, but everyone did what he was supposed to do. It was a tribute to the employees. They did what had to be done to get the plant cleaned out.

"On November 11, after the big meeting, I met with my group. Throughout the whole thing Biggar and Kennedy kept saying, 'The most important thing is to take care of our employees.' If people wanted to go home, we were to let them go and someone would cover their areas.

"Later that day Dave Kennedy asked me to be a part of a personnel placement committee. I was to try to get people placed elsewhere in IBM or outside. We hired a job-search firm to help employees look outside of IBM or to set up their own businesses. I attended a three-day training session on how to do this.

"I knew what I was going to do when IBM finally left Greencastle," Joe Taylor said. "My mother lives in Greencastle and she's not well. It wasn't fair to go off just for my own benefit and be selfish. I wasn't in great financial shape, but I thought I could get another job locally. On that very day I made my decision. I'm fifty-one years old and I decided to retire and find another job so I can take care of my mother. Since I knew what I was going to do, I could devote my time to helping other people decide what they were going to do."

"These were very trying times for our people," Taylor continued. "Families were on the verge of breaking up because one wanted to move and the other didn't. Some people were not eligible for retirement and wanted to relocate close to home, but in those places IBM didn't have jobs available. There were many heartaches and it was a very sad time to live through.

"One day a manager came into my office and started crying. He could have retired, but he wasn't ready to. It was really tearing him up inside. He wanted someone to make the decision for him. But no one could. Finally he decided to relocate, and he's happy that he did."

People began to leave in January and February. Word began to filter back to Greencastle about who was happy and who wasn't. Sometimes the wife was happy, but not the husband, and vice versa. Some decided to resign from IBM and return to Greencastle.

"From November until late February Kennedy held two staff meetings each day," Taylor said. "Twice a day he would ask, 'What are our people's problems?' He wanted all of us, including himself, to establish a close rapport with our people to help them through this."

On January 31, 1987, many of the retirees left. On February 27, the second group of retirees left. Throughout the period, many others were leaving to relocate. By the third week of February the plant was down to a skeleton crew.

"The Government Has Absolutely No Compassion" Within a few weeks of the announcement a large area of the plant was set up like a job fair. The company brought in representatives

from its other locations and functions in which there were job openings. An office area was set up, and once an employee decided about his or her interests, the company flew families out for a survey trip.

Sherry McMains' first instinct was to relocate to another IBM facility. "Managers handed out preference sheets to us," she said. "They told us which facilities had openings and asked us to select three preferences. Unfortunately, the close facilities had no openings, so it meant we'd have to move a considerable distance away.

"I made my selections and my husband and I took a survey trip at company expense to Mechanicsburg late in December. The company organized survey trips for everyone who considered relocating. They really rolled out the red carpet for us."

Still, Sherry's family was from Greencastle, as was that of her husband. Their daughter is the only grandchild on her side of the family. "It's very important to us," she said, "to have our daughter raised close to her family."

Then just after Christmas Sherry's husband Dan was approached about a job at corporate headquarters for Public Service of Indiana, where he worked. He got a pay raise, an opportunity for a better job, and would not have to relocate.

"So, on New Year's Day," said Sherry, "I called my immediate manager who had been so helpful to me since the announcement and told him that due to emotional ties and my husband's job, I was going to resign.

"I had started at IBM in 1983 as a secretary," Sherry explained, "and later became a secretary specialist, then a senior administrative specialist. I was promoted again to an associate systems and procedures analyst, in which position I helped to develop and maintain an on-line system and procedures for audits. It was really wonderful. I felt good because we were helping with audits at other sites and I felt I really knew what I was doing.

"In 1986 they asked me to teach other people. I found that to be very satisfying. I'd once given a presentation to one hundred or more people. I really enjoyed helping people learn. Managers would call me up and ask me how to do things, so I felt really good. My manager once asked me, 'Sherry, why didn't you ever consider becoming a teacher?'

"After thinking about what he said, I decided that I could contribute a lot to education. I never graduated from college, so I'm taking the $5,000 retraining money that IBM offered to employees who resign and I'm going back to school to get a degree in education. I want to teach high school or college business and computer education. I'm so excited!"

She continued. "I got a temporary job in February working for the federal government. I took a 48 percent cut in pay. My husband and I were interviewed for the *Wall Street Journal*. They printed that I took a 20 percent cut in pay, but Dan told the guy that, not me. Boy, did that reporter do a lousy job. We spent a combined three hours with him and he printed one sentence.

"Anyway, I've decided not to work for the government for the rest of my life. The pay is lousy. At IBM they make sure you get the education you need to do a job. Where I work now, they basically said to me, 'Here's the job; here's the end result; you figure out yourself how to get there.'

"At IBM managers and co-workers treat you like a human being. They always listened to my ideas. They advised me career-wise. They were all very supportive. At IBM I was an individual. My ideas were appreciated. I could present an idea or ask questions and I never felt embarrassed.

"At IBM my standard was that if I did a good job and put forth an effort, it would be an advantage to me either in terms of a career advancement or greater wages.

"Now at the government I'm not allowed to be myself like I was at IBM. When you do something wrong, they are not patient with you in government like at IBM. At IBM, if you make a mistake, they expect you to learn from it. They don't reprimand you. They sit you down and say, 'This is how you fix it.' The government on the other hand gives no counseling and has absolutely no compassion."

"I Could Have Had a Great Job"   Daniel Webster is twenty-four and lives in Brazil, Indiana, nearby to Greencastle. His father worked for many years for IBM Greencastle, and Dan took a job in 1985 with the National Parts Center operation in Greencastle.

With the plant closing, Dan's father, who is forty-nine, considered whether or not to retire. His father and mother discussed the matter extensively. His father said that when he decides to retire, he doesn't want to have anything to worry about, but now he still has one child to put through college. So he relocated.

Dan took a survey trip to Mechanicsburg. The job offered him as a parts analyzer was an advance from his Greencastle position. "I had a chance to move," he said. "I could have had a great job."

Dan, however, was going to college nights while working at IBM. He saw IBM's offer of retraining assistance as an opportunity to finish college and to go into teaching. "Some people have tried to discourage me from going into teaching by complaining about teachers' low salaries," he said, "but I want to be involved in coaching and the benefits are good in teaching."

So Dan's decision was different from his father's. He decided to stay in Brazil, Indiana, to finish school, and then go into teaching. "I wanted to spend my life with the people I knew," he concluded.

"I Like to Believe"   Dick Callahan had been considering retiring before the announcement of Greencastle's closing. He had twenty-one years with the company, and under the old retirement plan he would have paid a penalty in his pension for retiring before age sixty. When the company improved the retirement package, it made it attractive for people under sixty like Dick to retire, and so he did. In all, of some 546 people who were eligible for retirement from Greencastle, approximately 450 did retire. In several instances retirees took the company's offered retraining allowance and prepared themselves for new careers.

"I think I'm really going to enjoy my retirement," Callahan said. "I raise cattle, but my farm isn't too big. I don't need a lot of money. I do woodworking as a hobby, play with computers, and I'm interested in a lot of things. I like to work on cars in the body shop, and I want to study music.

"IBM had a training fund for spouses of employees. Because I was getting ready to retire, my wife went back to school on IBM's spouses training fund.

"I don't know anyone who has said that IBM treated them badly. I'm thankful, especially when I think what could have happened. At a plant in a nearby town, they just closed the whole plant down and gave the employees nothing.

"The big point here is how IBM took care of the people. The company truly realizes that it is no better than the people who work for it. I like to believe that someone at the top in the corporation is making decisions with people in mind. I know that the management committee of IBM and the board of directors don't know Dick Callahan, but I'd like to believe that they felt that what they did in Greencastle was in the best interest of all the people—of all the Dick Callahans who work for IBM.

"Other IBM employees around the country look at what happened at Greencastle and say, 'If they treated

Dick Callahan right, they treat me right.' People know what's
being done for them by the company."

Summary of Significant Points

■ In today's environment corporations are plagued with
tough competition, takeovers, mergers, acquisitions, consol-
idations, reorganizations, and shut downs. Some companies
announce bad news over the PA system, some hire consultants
to give employees the news, other hand out pink slips with
a final paycheck and usher employees out the door. There
are better ways.

■ Closing a plant may be more difficult for employees then
remissioning, but a committed company can minimize the
problems and maintain the support and loyalty of its people.

■ A company's commitment to its employees can be demonstrated by providing several options for them. These options
included transferring to another site, taking a generous early
retirement package, and resigning. Employees who chose
either of the latter two options were also given double separation pay, financial assistance in finding a new job, training al-
lowances, and compensation for increased commuting costs.

■ Effective communication helps employees to make a transition. The closing should be announced to all at the same
time to avoid damaging rumors, and direct supervisors have
a key role in facilitating the transition with those employees
who report to them.

■ What a company can gain from this sort of process if properly and compassionately executed: (1) increased loyalty to
the company on the part of managers and employees directly
affected by the shutdown; (2) a do-things-right attitude
among its own managers, thereby reinforcing a culture that
stresses excellence in everything the company does; and (3)
the support of employees not directly affected by the closing,
since they know it could happen to them and have confidence
that they'd also be treated well.

GREENCASTLE
AFTER THE CLOSING

Chapter Four

Battleship Gray "Two events stand out in my life," said Bobby Albright, mayor of Greencastle, Indiana. "The first is the day the Japanese bombed Pearl Harbor. I compare what happened at Pearl Harbor to what happened here in Greencastle on November 11, 1986, when IBM said it would close the plant."

The mayor sat in his small and cluttered office on the second floor of a somewhat ill-kept cement-block building in downtown Greencastle. His desk was a confusion of papers and books. The floor was carpetless, the windows lacked drapes, and a bare fluorescent light dangled from the ceiling.

Ironically, the mayor exulted in his austere surroundings. "There's no graft in Greencastle," he said, indicating his bare office. "There're no under-the-table dealings. What city officials make a month is what they get. There's no Mafia in Greencastle."

"On November 11," he continued, "Mayor Jerry Warren called me at 11:00 A.M. and said that at 1:00 P.M. the city council was going to have a meeting with IBM officials. Jerry is on the economics faculty at DePauw and he has a very bad heart condition. There was no way he could have lived through this closing with his bad heart, so he resigned after IBM made the announcement. I became mayor after he resigned.

"When I arrived at City Hall at 1:00 P.M. on the eleventh, I knew something was up because in marched the big tin soldiers from IBM. Normally when we meet with IBM it's just the little tin soldiers—the plant managers—but for this meeting they brought in people from division headquarters and from New York, so I knew something big was happening. They told us IBM would be closing down Greencastle in early March 1987."

Just a few hours earlier Dave and Charley had met with employees in the Greencastle plant. In his talk Biggar had no sooner finished listing the benefits available to those who chose to retire or resign from IBM rather than move, than he told the assembly of employees what the council was being told, that IBM had not forgotten the community. To minimize the effects of its departure the company took some extraordinary steps. It offered to donate its 260-acre site and 350,000-square-foot building to the town to help attract new business. Also, an IBM executive was made available full time to help the town attract new business. The company promised a $1.5 million contribution to help local government offset the loss of tax revenue and help with plant maintenance. Finally, the company offered to continue contributions to the town's major charitable drive, the United Way, for three years after the plant closed at the same level as its corporate and employee contributions had been running (approximately $150,000 per year). IBM had encouraged its people to contribute to the community, so that almost 70 percent of the United Way contributions in Greencastle came from IBM and its employees.

"Tuesday's sky was battleship gray," Jonathan Reiskin of the *Indianapolis News* began his coverage of the Greencastle closing, "when this city of 8,500 suffered a direct hit."

Greencastle's business community was very dependent on IBM. To make the point, Dave Kennedy recounted a personal experience the main features of which were often cited by other people in Greencastle from their own lives.

"I moved back to Greencastle in 1966," Dave said, "after having been away for a number of years. I went into the local appliance store to buy a stove, and the proprietor began to question me about how I would pay for it. When I told him that I wanted to pay by check, he told me that it wasn't possible for him to deliver the stove until the following week. Then I mentioned that I just started a new job at IBM. He looked up and said to me, 'I'll deliver that stove this afternoon.' "

Those of his customers with jobs at IBM, the appliance dealer thought, were suitable for credit. They had stable employment with a company which would meet its payroll regularly. When IBM announced its intention to leave, local newspapers noted that local businesses would suffer substantially.

In addition to the impact on local merchants, significant damage from the closing was suffered by the town's school system. Five days before IBM's announcement the school system took the final steps for a substantial building project: it sold over $3 million in bonds to build a new middle school and to add 22,000 square feet to the high school.

"It's peculiar the way it happened," said Jim Peck, the Greencastle superintendent of schools. "On November 11, I had to go to a funeral. Some close friends had lost their son in an automobile crash and my wife and I were leaving for Terre Haute at noon. That morning I got a call from the mayor, who asked me to come to City Hall after noon for an important meeting with IBM people. But I said I couldn't make it. When I got back from Terre Haute that afternoon late, I called the mayor and he told me the news. I couldn't believe it! It was as if I had to deal with two deaths in one day.

"What really disturbed me was that we had no warning whatsoever. If we had known about the plant closing on November 5 instead of November 11, we could have canceled the bond sale. Currently a homeowner in Greencastle pays $6.34 per $1,000 valuation in taxes. With the new bond issue and IBM moving out, we are afraid it may go to $10.65 per thousand in two years. IBM paid 21 percent of the town's taxes, and with IBM moving out, the population in the area is also dropping considerably.

"Last year we had three local meetings to discuss the building project for the middle school. No one opposed it! I think it might have been the only school building project in this state built without one single letter to the newspaper editor opposing it. Now we don't need it and can't afford it. Our enrollment was twenty-five hundred. It has dropped to sixteen hundred with the closing of IBM."

"Another thing IBM didn't consider was the full implications of turning over its $1.5 million gift to the town. In Indiana, the school corporation does not fall under city government. Hence, the money IBM was going to give to the town went only to the town, not to the schools.

"So three weeks after the announcement I went to talk to Dave Kennedy and Ken Current, the IBM executive who was detailed to the town to help it adjust, and they agreed to have $450,000 turned over to the schools."

But the loss to Greencastle was more than financial. IBM employees had been very much involved with the schools. Their children had participated in most school activities. In 1986 the girls' soccer team from Greencastle went to the state championship. Nine of the twelve girls on the team were children of IBM employees. In the same year the school's debating team won a state award. It also was composed largely of IBMers' children.

The company itself was supportive of the school system. In 1985 IBM sponsored a week-long seminar in New Jersey for school officials from all over the nation. Seven people from Greencastle attended, including Jim Peck. "It was one of the finest programs we've ever gone to," he said. "They paid for everything except our travel. At the seminar they told us about the IBM management philosophy and how it would be applicable to schools.

"IBM also built a special lab in the Greencastle plant for our schoolchildren. We gave two of our teachers partial leaves of absence so that IBM could train them to use the lab. Children would attend the lab one day a week for a six-week period. When IBM closed Greencastle, it gave us the equipment and paid the teachers' salaries."

The continual turnover of people at the IBM plant, especially of executives and professionals moving in and out of Greencastle on assignments of only a few years, brought a continual inflow of new pupils to the schools. Their parents were generally supportive of education and the school system. IBM employees knew from their own experience the importance of education to keeping up in an environment in which business conditions and technology are continually changing. The company's tradition of continual training and career shifts emphasized the significance of a firm grounding in the schools for a person's future. IBMers and their children brought to Greencastle a seriousness about learning that derived from personal experience with its importance.

Coupled with DePauw University, whose faculty and students have often traveled widely, many IBM employees contributed a breadth of view and understanding to the Greencastle public schools. "The really good thing about having IBM in the community," commented Gary Lemon, chairman of the Department of Economics at DePauw, "was that IBM rotated people in from other areas. That was real good, because it allowed us to have more variety of people in our community."

As a result, Peck said, "the children who are here permanently have learned not to treat people as outsiders. Our kids have adapted well to people coming and going. We have a much broader perspective."

But could that perspective be maintained with IBM gone from Greencastle? Jim Peck didn't say.

"We're Not Going to Be Whipped by This" Dan Doan is president of the First Citizen's Bank of Greencastle and was until recently head of its chamber of commerce. On November 11,

1986, his eight-year-old daughter, home from school for lunch, asked him, "Daddy, is it sometimes okay to tell secrets? If it is okay, I want to tell you, but I'm not supposed to tell anyone."

What she wanted to tell him was that one of her schoolmates had just phoned to say that she was moving away from Greencastle because the IBM plant was going to be closed.

"I smiled at my daughter, but I dismissed the idea," Doan said. "I told myself, 'There's no way IBM could be leaving Greencastle.' I had attended a quality of life forum some months earlier at which various management people in the Greencastle area gave reports on their respective companies. Dave assured everyone that everything was going truly well at IBM Greencastle. But I also remember him saying, 'Granted, anything can change.'

"On the afternoon of November 11, Dick called me to tell me the news. I was shell-shocked. So much so, I mixed myself a Bloody Mary. Within the next two hours I began to get telephone calls from the media.

"It was the first time in my life that I had to deal with television people. I think they had decided in advance the tone of the story and wanted to make it a tragedy."

Richard Andis had been loaned on a full-time basis by IBM to Greencastle in August 1986 to help set up an economic development and support center for the town. Immediately upon IBM's announcement he decided to retire from IBM to continue to devote himself full time to the economic development of the community. Even though IBM's leaving was a heavy blow to Greencastle, Dick Andis had great confidence in the town and its people, and saw great opportunities for them. On the afternoon of November 11 he called Dan Doan, and before the day was out Greencastle's business leaders were preparing for the town's life after IBM. "Now it's leadership time," Andis said. He was already putting his decades of experience as an IBM executive into an adjustment plan for the town. Andis wanted Greencastle to do what an IBM unit would do in a business crisis: set goals and act immediately.

Doan and Andis called a meeting of the town's leadership for the next morning. Some forty people attended. Wisely, Doan and Andis first let people vent their dismay, anger, and frustrations. Then they all made a commitment to move ahead. Within a day of IBM's announcement, Greencastle had developed an organization of its leading citizens and had set goals for the town's immediate future.

"For years we had been complaining in Greencastle," said Dick Andis, "that we didn't have enough building space in town. Now we had the biggest, grandest, most spectacular building and a pretty big strip of land as well. It was time to start correcting some of Greencastle's problems."

"In a sense," Dan Doan said, "that meeting represented IBM's funeral and burial at Greencastle, not twenty-four hours after the town was told of IBM's decision. And that meeting represented the resurrection of Greencastle. We all felt much better after the meeting."

Jim Peck attended the meeting as well. His involvement demonstrated the clear conviction of Greencastle's business that the town's school system is a significant part of its economic resources.

"At the meeting on the twelfth," Peck said, "several IBM executives spoke about the move. After they left, all the people at the meeting said, 'We're not going to be whipped by this.'"

From the moment the IBM executives left the Greencastle leaders' meeting on November 12, a subtle but crucial change occurred in Greencastle's relationship to IBM. For the corporation the issue continued to be how to handle the closing of its facility. But for the community the issue became "What next?" For the townspeople the question now was: what could IBM contribute to help make a renewed Greencastle a reality?

Peck continued. "The people of Greencastle are resilient. We'll recover from IBM's closing. We did well before IBM came here, and we're here after IBM has gone. The city has put together a solid team to sell Greencastle to other companies, and with our new building project, we'll have one of the finest school systems in the state. We'll have excellent facilities, which will be a real drawing card."

Already, to Peck's mind, the school bond issue, which would have been canceled had IBM given the town only a few days additional notice, was emerging not as a burden but as an advantage in attracting new business to the town.

"I don't think IBM could have done anything differently," said Mayor Albright. "Some corporations close plants down with a week's notice. We were given three or four months. I think we were fortunate. I don't think more advanced notice would have helped."

Gary Lemon of DePauw echoed the judgment. "Assuming that we had known for a year, there's still no way to prepare for it. It was better the way IBM did it. They hit us and left—it was all over.

"If a company is going to pull out of a community," he continued, "I'd rather have IBM pull out than other big companies because IBM says, 'We'll take care of you.' They paid us handsomely to pull out."

"I think the way our community has handled this has been wonderful," Jim Peck concluded. "No one has any antagonism toward IBM or its people."

What Peck said was largely true, most people expressed no antagonism. But as we shall see below, there was some bitter feeling from a perhaps unexpected source— DePauw University—and for surprising reasons.

"I'm Pretty Scared"   IBM's departure from Greencastle had left the community with some hard choices to make about its future. Because of the way IBM conducted its closing, the community was not left devastated and without recourse. Instead, the town was forced to decide in what direction it wanted to channel its efforts and to what uses to put its resources. These kinds of choices, about what sort of future to aim for, are daunting, because the outcome is so uncertain. The need to make choices also brings out the most deeply rooted convictions of people about what kind of community it is in which they wish to live.

"I'm pretty scared," said Mayor Albright, "about doing the right thing for the community. The decisions the city council and I make will have a lasting impact on the town long after I'm gone."

Perhaps surprisingly, IBM's offer, which seemed most generous, had become the focal point of controversy over the town's future.

"An interesting thing happened to me," said Jim Peck, "as a result of all the publicity we were getting around the country. The Chicago *Tribune* published a story on the Greencastle closing. In the story was mentioned IBM's gift of the plant to the town. A man from Illinois called me to say that a large automotive company had just given his town notice that it would close its big plant in eighteen months. He asked me how Greencastle had gotten IBM to contribute the plant to the town, since he thought that was a wonderful thing.

"I told him," Peck continued, "that we didn't get IBM to do anything. We didn't ask for it. It was offered by IBM to us."

"I knew that the city council had to take a stand on whether or not to accept IBM's offer of the plant," Mayor Albright said. "We had a lot of heated discussions about it. Some people wanted to use the money IBM was donating to the city for streets and things like that, but I felt we should pay off the town's debt to get us solvent again and use what remained for economic development so that we could attract jobs and increase our tax base."

Some people argued that the plant would be an economic albatross around the town's neck. No other company would want it, they said. IBM was only donating it to the town to avoid having to maintain it and pay taxes on it, they insisted. Initial estimates of maintenance costs were almost a million dollars a year plus security for the plant. The town would go broke trying to maintain the plant, it was said.

But three-quarters of the taxes IBM paid to the town on the plant were not on its land and buildings, but on the value of its inventory, all of which had been moved out. Hence IBM's offer of the plant to the town and its $1.5 million payment were not simply a cheap way to avoid taxes and dump the responsibility for the plant on the town.

In addition, Richard Taylor, an IBM executive involved in the transition, put together a report for the city council on how to minimize maintenance costs and brought the expected maintenance and security down to $300,000 per year.

As the weeks passed and the city council debated, IBM grew impatient. The company then offered an additional $200,000 to the town if it would make its decision by a certain date. In December the town created an industrial commission and established a fund into which contributions such as IBM promised could be funneled without going into the city's general fund.

"We knew that we had to take a stand on whether or not to accept IBM's offer," Albright continued. "We knew that the corporate world is a vicious place. We also knew that IBM had been compassionate and wanted to take care of its people and the community. But if we pushed

IBM too hard, or stalled too long, we knew they'd fire back at us. We had to make a decision."

"There Is Nothing Positive About the Greencastle Closing"   Robert Bottoms is president of DePauw University and deeply concerned about Greencastle's future. His campus is highlighted by a lovely Gothic quadrangle constructed of Indiana limestone, surrounded by more modern classrooms, labs, and dormitories. In the older building, which contains his office, broad corridors and staircases of marble suggest the permanence and beauty of the campus.

Unlike the University of Colorado at Boulder, DePauw has no close relations with the IBM facility in its community. But the university is very much aware of its former neighbor. Without exception, DePauw people speak favorably of IBM's stay in Greencastle. But there is criticism of how it left.

"IBM took over Greencastle when it moved here in the 1950s," Bottoms said. "To a great extent they made the town what it is. They took the best-educated people, and now they are leaving and taking those people, at least many of them, with them. Once IBM pulled out, there was nothing left here. There is nothing positive about IBM leaving Greencastle.

"Usually a town gets some signals that a company is going to close a plant down. There weren't any signals from IBM. Since I've been here, the plant was expanded twice. There were no signals to give us concern.

"A town this size doesn't have a lot of flexibility, so a company has a greater responsibility to it. When IBM closed, our personnel department was swamped with applications. We hired a few people, but there's no way we could hire the number of people who applied. IBM had to offer people transfers and retraining once they pulled out. If IBM hadn't, it would have been a tragedy."

Several years ago Greencastle established a group to look at its future. Called the Greencastle 2001 Committee, it had representatives of the town, the business community (including the IBM plant), and the schools and university. Gary Lemon represented DePauw on the committee.

"It's funny," he said, "we never dreamed that IBM wouldn't be here in the year 2001.

"On November 11 a friend came up to me and said, 'Did you hear the news? IBM is shutting down?'

"I thought it was a joke," said Lemon, "so I asked him, 'What's the punch line?' But there wasn't any punch line, and it wasn't a joke. The closing was a real shock to all of us."

Even though Lemon credits IBM with being generous in how it pulled out of Greencastle, like Bottoms, he has great reservations about the direction in which IBM seemed to have nudged Greencastle's future.

"What we had here with IBM was almost ideal. We had a good corporate citizen with a large payroll. We had no smokestacks, and we had lots of white-collar workers.

"Now we have almost 250 acres of an industrial park to be developed. The community seems to be interested in just filling the buildings by getting new firms. The new jobs will probably be for blue-collar workers. The people trying to attract new firms to Greencastle are focusing on companies in the automotive parts business, and Greencastle is probably ideally situated to be the nub of that business.

"But the bad thing is that then Greencastle will become tied more to business cycles in that industry. There will be layoffs and unemployment. The blue-collar/white-collar mix will change in the town, with more blue-collar workers when the country as a whole is going the other way. We will be going backward—against the tide of history.

Greencastle will survive, but it will not be as good as it was before."

Bottoms and Lemon, the intellectuals in Greencastle, think differently than others in the community. Their view is much longer term. They worry less about having jobs for people immediately, and more about the kind of town which will ultimately result. They are aware of the change toward a service economy in the nation and are afraid that Greencastle will be taken in the wrong direction—back toward a manufacturing orientation. They fault IBM for not helping the town think through its future, and they blame the company for having, probably inadvertently, nudged Greencastle toward manufacturing by giving the town its plant.

In essence, they argue that IBM closed the facility because its business had changed. IBM was adjusting to a different situation.

But how has Greencastle been handling its own adjustment? Did it accept the challenge and prepare to meet a more demanding future? Perhaps it did not.

Even the great majority of those displaced from the IBM facility resisted change. Most of those eligible to retire did so, almost a majority of the plant's work force. It can be argued that they chose not to adapt, but to drop out. Many others chose not to relocate but instead resigned, hanging on to what they could in Greencastle. A small group saw the closing as an opportunity to leave IBM to enter careers they preferred to working for IBM, and so did adapt. Another small minority of the plant's work force chose to accept the challenge of a changing business world and move on with the company.

IBM moved because a changing world forced it to. The town itself, though it acted promptly and avoided the trap of despondency, turned backward economically, its critics insist, by trying to obtain what so many other Indiana cities and towns already have had for decades: a piece of the nation's shrinking automotive industry. Greencastle seems to be choosing less to adapt to the new world than to simply try to cope with its immediate problem. Essentially they see Greencastle as trying to preserve, rather than to create, and in so doing being likely to experience serious slippage in many areas. The town's school system has no hope of attracting the sort of highly motivated students it is losing. The professional ranks in the community are not going to be replaced by the autoparts companies. This shrinking back into the commonplace is what is most disquieting to some about Greencastle after IBM's departure.

To some, the vacant IBM facility has become a symbol of a blue-collar community, and therefore an object of derision to those who have a different vision of Greencastle's future.

"Now the IBM plant is our headache," Bottoms lamented. "Maybe they should have bulldozed it down."

"We'll Be Home Free"   While the intellectuals worry about Greencastle's long-term direction, its business and political leaders are busy trying to build a new economic base for the community. After lengthy discussion, the Greencastle city council voted to accept IBM's offer of its plant. The town's industrial council took possession of the facility under the terms of Indiana's 1981 Economic Development Act, empowering the council to manage or dispose of the property.

The Greencastle Development Center is spearheading the effort to attract new employers. Associated with the center are the mayor, two bankers, the city attorney, a local engineer, a representative of DePauw, one of Public Service of Indiana (the electric power utility), and a loaned executive from IBM. Dick Andis, formerly of IBM, heads the center.

The council identified a key element of Greencastle's work force as farmers who are also looking for industrial jobs. "We have many unskilled and semi-skilled people who need manufacturing jobs," said Dick Andis. "This area is not predominantly a white-collar community."

So the city is trying to attract companies which can employ such a work force. Conscious of the risk of getting too closely tied to a single employer, as Greencastle now believes it was to IBM, the community is looking for three companies to employ some three hundred people each, rather than one company to employ more than nine hundred, as IBM did.

"My feelings," said Dick Andis, "are that if we find a client for the plant within a year, we'll be home free. We've gotten worldwide publicity for Greencastle from the IBM closing. We've gotten a lot of inquiries about the site, without putting any money into advertising. Even if we don't find a client soon, we've planned out a scenario with four different avenues of attracting one. I can't understand some people's attitudes," he added. "I've seen some beat-down people since the closing. Why?"

Mayor Albright commented, "Right now my main concern is to get something in that building. I think positively about Big Blue, but we've reached a point now where we're saying, 'To hell with IBM. We're going to make out a hell of a lot better without them.'"

Soon thereafter a company that produces automotive parts began construction of a facility on part of the former IBM land and will hire two hundred people. In three to five years the company expects to employ five to seven hundred people.

The IBM plant is under contract to an apparel distributor which will employ several hundred people. Japanese auto parts manufacturers are in the process of locating facilities in Greencastle. The community lost 985 jobs when

IBM closed. Within a year it had prospects for 1,360 jobs in initial hiring and 2,500 to 2,700 over the longer term.

Summary of Lessons Learned
■ Closing a plant is tough not only on employees but also on a community as a whole because a good company becomes a part of the community in many important ways.
■ For many communities a plant shutdown has become a reality. Yet few communities are given advance notice and even fewer are recompensed upon a company's departure. The community dislocation and poor public relations for the company involved can be avoided.
■ Carefully prepared communication by company executives with the community can make the transition less troublesome.
■ Given some support, a community can be fairly resilient.
■ A community can resent even a supportive and generous company if the company does not help the community plan for its economic future.
■ The press generally makes maintaining good public relations during a shutdown more difficult by emphasizing the negative aspects of the situation.
■ A company doesn't give financial and other support to a community just to help it to feel better about a closing. Instead, assistance is part of an overall concept of corporate responsibility which should be adjusted according to the size of the company's role in the community. The company's ideal should be to be a good corporate citizen.
■ What does a company gain from a careful and supportive closing of a facility? (1) an enhanced public image; (2) a position of strength in lobbying with government authorities about various matters including legislation, since it is a good corporate citizen; and (3) elevated status for its own employees in the communities in which they live, since the company conducts itself so well.

MOVING A SITE: THE WESTLAKE EXPERIENCE

Chapter Five

Even though IBM as a whole was in the throes of a major business slump some aspects of the business were expanding. Among them was the Federal Systems Division, which does work for the federal government, and in particular one of FSD's programming units located at Westlake, California. The unit does systems development for the Air Force, and had outgrown its location. As Boulder was being remissioned, Westlake was looking for room to grow. So it was that the Westlake unit found a new home at Boulder as part of the Boulder remissioning.

In the process, what had seemed a straightforward move became the occasion for complex issues of an individual's relocation and new careers. The movement from Westlake to Boulder became one of the more significant management challenges encountered by an IBM facility manager in recent years.

"What If the Company Is a Government Contractor and the Government Cancels the Contract?"   In discussing IBM's full-employment practice with me, an executive at another firm objected that full employment might work for IBM but that firms in his line of work could not do it. "What if your company is a government contractor, like mine is," he asked, "and the government cancels the contract? You couldn't do anything but lay the people off."

At the time the point seemed irrefutable, but I later learned exactly what had happened to Westlake at its inception. The facility was established in 1968 to do programming for the manned space laboratory, only to have the program canceled as the Vietnam War expanded. Several hundred new IBMers, hired for the project, were without work. Yet none were laid off. Instead, the corporation found new assignments for all who wished them. For two to three years after the contract was canceled, IBM bussed about two hundred people daily to work in the San Bernardino Valley.

With this experience in mind, the company thereafter was very reluctant to allow the facility to expand its work force. FSD and Westlake in particular were asked to manage in an especially careful way so that nothing like this happened again.

Partly as a result of this experience, and partly because IBM is wary of dispersing its resources in too many small facilities, the Westlake site was always a temporary one for the corporation, and the employees were always aware of that. By 1986 Westlake was nearly a twenty-year-old temporary site. In recent years it had performed well, its business was growing, and many employees at Westlake had concluded that the site was secure for years to come.

Over its life Westlake held a number of government contracts and developed a reputation as a fine unit in its special areas. But the business remained volatile, with large projects sometimes downsized or canceled. For example, in 1972 there were more than six hundred people at Westlake, and only some three hundred soon thereafter. For IBM each significant shift in Westlake's fortunes caused either scurrying for new work for people if contracts were down, or for more people to perform the additional work when contracts were up.

The IBM programming facility at Westlake is located in a picture-perfect community nestled in the Conejo Valley just north and west of Los Angeles. The area was once a large ranch and was developed as a unit in the 1950s around a large lake. It is a community of fine homes, quiet tree-lined streets, and attractive parks. Mountains rise in the distance, and Malibu Beach and the Pacific Ocean beckon only a few miles to the south. The climate is warm year round, and skies are generally fair. Housing prices have soared over the years as the community has become a much-desired place to live.

IBM occupied a multiple-story office building which by mid-1986 housed some five hundred employees in increasingly crowded quarters. But for all its attraction as a place to live, Westlake was far removed from the centers of action in its own business. IBM's Federal Systems Division has most of its facilities and people on the East Coast, especially in the Washington, D.C., metropolitan area. When Westlake became overburdened with work, or when its contracts with the government required close coordination with facilities in the east, the skies filled with IBMers traveling from the East to help out in the West. Yet it was often difficult to get FSD people to relocate to Westlake.

Because Westlake was far away from the centers of division activity, it became for many ambitious people a place to be avoided. "Too far from the action to be a good place to build a career," they said.

Deciding to Relocate the Facility   Don Upton was an executive in FSD with a position in the Washington, D.C., area. In 1985 he accepted an appointment as site manager at Westlake, arriving in California to assume his duties in February 1986.

The problems confronting him were substantial. That they were the problems of success—for the unit's work was growing rapidly—was a source of satisfaction and opportunity, but they were difficult nonetheless. The unit was outgrowing its space. Career opportunities for those in the unit seemed to be limited because of their distance from other FSD facilities and because of the small size of Westlake. Employee attitude surveys indicated that people at Westlake were more pessimistic about their opportunities for growth and promotion than other people elsewhere in the division were. Overhead expenses associated with staff functions, security, employee benefits, and other items were high because they were shared over so small an employee population. Additional programming and other resources, such as were available in the East or in larger western facilities, were absent at Westlake. These issues were discussed with senior IBM executives, and the decision to move the business unit to a major IBM facility rather than build a new facility in Westlake was made.

"Essentially," Don said, "the site was too small, and the FSD support structure was back east. At a major IBM site we wouldn't be so constrained by the risk of the cancellation of a contract." Work could most likely be found for people released from a canceled project, so that Don's unit would be allowed to increase its staff more freely, and grow in new business areas.

Also, Don wanted people who worked in his unit to be able to move up in IBM without having to relocate. At Westlake this was simply not possible. As a result, too many people plateaued in their careers. Some who wanted to move up but were reluctant to relocate stayed in jobs they had outgrown. In other cases, employees who did not relocate were not exposed to the kinds of experiences which made them ready for advancement.

Finally, by going to a larger site, Don's unit could draw on greater staff resources, share overhead services, and thereby avoid greater costs in Westlake. By moving, the unit could explore new business opportunities that would not have been practical in Westlake.

As Don and his staff investigated possible sites, the remissioning of Boulder was being decided and the president of FSD strongly urged him to consider Boulder. Suddenly a site had opened which met Don's criteria. There was ample office space for the Westlake unit. With the remissioning of Boulder to programming, there would be substantial additional resources available. And there were much larger support systems at Boulder. For example, in order to support six distinct business missions from several different divisions, Boulder had a substantial security system; personnel office; building maintenance unit; and set of employee health, exercise, and activities programs. Don's unit could rely on all these large systems at Boulder, thereby greatly improving the services provided beyond those possible at Westlake, yet reducing the unit's overhead.

Further, Boulder was much closer to the unit's key client, which was located at Colorado Springs. Because it was only a two-hour drive from Boulder, IBM engineers might more readily interface with their Air Force counterparts. And for the unit's customer who was in Southern California, some offered the opinion that it would be easier for the client to take a plane to Boulder than to drive on the freeways to Westlake.

Planning the Move   The move from Westlake to Boulder was planned in great detail. Two broad considerations interacted continually: scheduling of business output, and people concerns. To meet the former, certain groups of employees had to be moved by certain dates, set up in their new surroundings, and able to continue work just as if they were in Westlake. Satellite communications reception dishes had to be transferred to Boulder at just the right time. And to minimize the adverse impact on employees and their families, some people were offered the option of moving by the end of August before the start of the new school year.

The management team discussed the situation of each employee with respect to the move. What were the circumstances of each individual's work and family? Who would go and who would stay? It appeared that roughly 60 percent of the work force at Westlake would transfer to Boulder.

Whenever possible, people were moved just as they completed an assignment so that they could begin something new upon their arrival at Boulder. The planning determined that there had to be a major move in October 1986, and the final one in January 1987. To get children in schools in September, a few people took advantage of the early move in August.

To facilitate the move at Boulder, a special transition team composed of Westlake, Boulder, and FSD headquarters personnel was established. The team handled office and other needs in order to reduce the pressure on those moving. Because of this support, the people who moved could devote their effort to the work of the unit, rather than getting established in their new offices.

The move was carried out successfully. Business continued without interruption. In October 1986, in the midst of the transition, a major delivery was made to the customer. But there were difficult spots, especially with respect to the movement of people. It proved difficult to persuade many people to transfer to Boulder. Despite management's conviction that the move was the best thing for both the business and the people, some employees at Westlake had considerable reservations. In the end, less than half of Westlake's personnel made the transition to Boulder.

Announcing the Move   On a Saturday in early June 1986, Don Upton, his management staff, and managers from FSD headquarters assembled in an IBM branch office in Southern California to plan the move. The unit would be expanding its size during the relocation. Each member of the planning team was committed to keep the decision in confidence to control rumors and misinformation. After an explanation of the rationale for the relocation decision, the group was divided into teams to plan various aspects of the move—a detailed schedule, customer and contractor considerations, personnel guidelines, community concerns, etc. By late Sunday night, the move had been planned.

Over the next four days, a smaller group of managers critiqued the move plans and fine-tuned them while other individuals began implementation activities such as preparing bulletin board announcements, preparing employee handouts, scheduling relocation briefings and the like.

The announcement was made on June 12, 1986. The events of that day were carefully orchestrated to ensure that everyone who needed to know about the relocation was informed. The day began at 6:30 A.M. for Don Upton and his key staff with briefings to the FSD president and the Air Force, the unit's customer. The business rationale was explained to the Air Force and assurances were given that IBM would meet its commitments. The FSD president announced the relocation to the Westlake managers at a luncheon. Don Upton also spoke, emphasizing that the move would be handled in a sensitive manner. All Westlake employees were informed at a meeting immediately following the luncheon. After the meeting each employee was given a package containing information about the Boulder community and the IBM facility. Each manager was asked to meet with his/her employees individually to understand their reaction and concerns. Over the next several days, many similar meetings were held to explain the move guidlelines, answer questions, and listen to employees' concerns.

Throughout the day on June 12 calls were made to other IBM executives in California to apprise them of the move. News of the relocation announcement was posted on IBM bulletin boards throughout the company. Don Upton had undertaken to move a unit of nearly five hundred people a thousand miles, increase its size while doing so, and continue its work without significant interruption or delay during the process. The decisions made, the task was now to implement them.

Jay Allen was personnel manager at Westlake, and also managed security and facilities. He played a key role in the planning and execution of the move. "I have thought a lot about the move since I transferred," he said. "People went through a lot. Many were very bitter and angry and had a hard time getting past that. I think you go through stages with things like this, similar to what they say about death and dying. The last one is acceptance. I hope people get there, accept the move, and go on, but many haven't."

"People reacted differently," said Ian Murray, a manager who later retired from IBM. "Some came out in tears, while others were so excited."

"I started with IBM at Westlake in 1968," an employee told us. "In 1976 I asked for a transfer to San Jose because I was in the process of getting a divorce and wanted to get away. Five years later I felt that I had been away from my children for too long, so I began to investigate jobs in Southern California. In 1985 I was hired at Westlake and started my new job there on May 1, 1986. Then six weeks later they made the announcement to close Westlake.

"My first reaction was hysterical laughter . . . I said to myself, 'This is the most ridiculous posture I've ever gotten myself into.' I just couldn't believe that they would hire me and then one month later close the facility down.

"After that it was very difficult for me to feel any permanence. I lived in an apartment and decided not to try to buy a place. I went to Boulder on a survey trip for two days and decided that I really wanted to stay in L.A. to be with my children. So I said to the company, 'Whatever you can find for me here in L.A. I'll do . . . it doesn't matter what.

"It was very upsetting for me, not knowing where I'd be working. I didn't know anything from June 1986 until February–March 1987. I always had this feeling that I wanted to be in a permanent place. I wanted things to get back to normal.

"I was never really worried about getting another job at IBM. I've worked for IBM for nineteen years and I've never seen a company do so much for its people. But I knew that if I didn't get my personal side under control—like a permanent place to live—then it would impact on the kind of job I'd do at work.

"I went out on three interviews, and I took a new job. I'm going to be putting an administrative system in a new organization. I feel pretty good about it. I do have some knowledge, but no experience in the department. I felt pretty good that another IBM organization could use the experience I had gained in another IBM facility."

IBM also held a briefing on the decision to move for local government officials and the press. A large number of people were invited. Three came. The mayor of Westlake did not attend, but sent an aide. After a brief statement was read there was only one comment from the tiny audience. A chamber of commerce representative offered to help IBM with the move and said that maybe the chamber could find a new employer for the IBM building. The entire meeting—refreshments, statement, comments, etc.—took less than forty-five minutes.

How very different this reaction was from that in Greencastle, Indiana. But in Westlake, IBM was only a small employer in the very large area of Southern California. Other companies employed far more people, even in Westlake, and jobs were not difficult to find in the area.

As a result, IBM took few of the steps which had made its departure from Greencastle so memorable. The plant was not given to the community; no executives were assigned to assist in the transition of the community; nothing was paid in lieu of taxes; no education grants to resignees and retirees were made; future contributions to charity were not offered. IBM departed from Westlake quietly, and the community hardly noticed.

"Don, Are You Sitting Down?"   The initial planning for the Westlake move had estimated that roughly 60 percent of West-

lake's people would relocate to Boulder. Over the summer months following the announcement, almost two hundred Westlakers decided not to relocate. It appeared that the initial estimate of attrition had been accurate, and that the plans which had been made would make the move to Boulder successful.

Then, about September 5, 1986, Don Upton received a call from Jay Allen. "Don," Jay began, "are you sitting down?"

The news was grim for Westlake's management. The IBM corporation was to announce a major early retirement incentive. Westlake, with a large population of employees near retirement age, was likely to be hit especially hard by persons taking the opportunity to retire, particularly since these employees would also receive separation pay associated with the relocation.

"That day was tougher for me than the day we made the announcement that we were moving to Boulder," said Don Upton.

The Air Force expressed concern that the FSD unit would be losing critical skills, but stressed that it would not permit any relaxation of the agreed-upon schedule of costs and deliveries.

The early retirement incentive affected individual employees in dramatic ways. Alice Cunningham had returned to work at forty, when her children were twelve and fourteen years of age. "That was eleven years ago," she told us. "I came to Westlake to do a good job. One of my goals at IBM was to work long enough to be able to retire from the company. When the move to Boulder was announced, I fell four years short of my goal. From that moment on I did not fall asleep at night and did not wake up the next morning without thinking about what I was going to do.

"For every solution I came up with, there was always an obstacle," she lamented. Her husband was eligible to retire from his employer, but could not get a position at Boulder. He did arrange a possible transfer to Tucson with his company, but she was told a position for her at the IBM facility in Tucson was unlikely.

A potential position in the L.A. area was all that remained, she continued, "but I don't want to drive on the freeways. The freeways are unbearable if you have to use them every day."

Jay Allen notes that "every employee who qualified under the relocation guidelines, even if placed in the L.A. basin, was given a moving and relocation allowance. That most chose not to move is another topic. Most are receiving excess commutation payments."

"In August some rumors started about a new early retirement plan," Alice continued. "Each day my hopes would rise and fall. I kept hoping that something would bail me out of this. My manager knew how stressed I was. Then in September he stopped by my office late one afternoon and said, 'I can't tell you anything, but all I want to say is that you qualify.' I knew just what he meant. That night was the first night since June 12 that I slept like a baby."

In the months that followed about eighty Westlake employees decided to accept the retirement incentive and forgo relocation to Boulder. Now the FSD unit stood to lose more than half its total personnel during the move. In this difficult situation Upton called upon many who were retiring and some who were transferring to other IBM units in L.A. to take a temporary assignment at Boulder. Without this cadre of experienced people the work might not have been completed as scheduled. By persuasion and appeals, management got almost one hundred persons to do temporary duty at Boulder. These people not only did much of the work of the unit during this time period but also trained new people to take over their work.

The permanent FSD unit at Boulder took

shape from several sources. People were hired into the unit from other functions at Boulder, that is, were redeployed into FSD. Others were transferred in from other FSD locations. Still others, who had transferred years ago from Boulder to Tucson in another division and wanted to return to Boulder, were invited to join FSD. Additionally, despite a corporate-wide freeze on hiring, the FSD unit moving from Westlake to Boulder was given an exception and permitted to hire critical skills from the outside for employment at Boulder. Lastly, FSDers who moved from Westlake were retrained for more responsible jobs at Boulder in the FSD unit. Because of retirements the opportunities which Don Upton had foreseen for younger people in the larger environment at Boulder materialized far more rapidly than he had anticipated.

In the end, of the 455 people at Westlake, 222 people moved with the project, 97 transferred elsewhere, 82 retired, and 54 resigned. Thus, of 455 people, 223 did not make the move.

Despite this heavy loss of personnel, the FSD unit made its scheduled deliveries to its customer and actually added a net one hundred people to its complement by a year following the announcement of the move. That is, in July 1987, the FSD unit at Boulder employed some six hundred people.

There were limitations which affected adversely both the ease of the move and its probability of success, and also threatened to undo much of the employee loyalty which the company had built over many years. Among the key limitations of the approach at Westlake were:

■ failure to anticipate the special retirement incentives and to plan for their impact (this was not primarily a failure of the site management, but a failure at a higher level where the retirement incentive was developed);
■ the impact of the Denver/Boulder labor market on the employment of working spouses;

■ failure to convince many employees that the business reasons given for the move to Boulder were compelling;

■ confusion about guidelines stemming from a less-than-strong middle management team.

These limitations are made clear by the loss to the FSD unit in Boulder of many employees who would have been valuable to the organization and who might well have benefitted from joining in the relocation.

Thorns Among the Roses   The movement of the Westlake operation is a remarkable story made possible by careful planning, establishment of key execution committees, and continual attention to the human side of business. But in the pressure of the move in progress, strains were evident.

"For weeks after the announcement," Alice Cunningham said, "people's work effort slowed to almost a halt. Nothing got done for work. I don't think they planned on that."

She added, "My perception is that the move was handled very heavy-handedly. After they made the announcement, they came back to every employee who was not going to move to Boulder and said, 'We're going to need your services for at least three months in Boulder, and then we'll send your packet out for another job within IBM.' "

Jay Allen does not believe that this is correct. He explains, "After the announcement, each manager was asked to sit down with her/his employees and talk about the relocation. There was a structured set of questions:

■ What is your reaction?

■ Do you think you will relocate?

■ If not, would you be willing to go on a temporary tour of duty to Boulder?

■ Do you have any family considerations we should try to accommodate?

■ Are there any questions you would like answered?
Managers were instructed that their major role in this interview was to listen. Never was placement made contingent on
a temporary assignment to Boulder."

Alice continued, "We were given to under-
stand that if we went on an interview and they liked you,
then this is all you had. Essentially we were told we had one
shot. We couldn't say, 'But I don't like that manager.' The
more sturdy among us didn't like this and reported it to
corporate. Local management changed that."

Jay Allen reports, "This is not correct. We
went through a number of interviews for many people. There
were no complaints to corporate and no corporate interven-
tion ever occurred on behalf of employees at Westlake."

Alice told us, "Then there was a rumor that
if we didn't help with the move by going to Boulder for three
to six months, we might not get our severance pay. This finally
cleared up as well. As time went on, more jobs opened up.
Maybe someone from higher up said, 'You better absorb these
people.'

"Companies will have to think about both
breadwinners in the future," Alice Cunningham explained,
"if they want their employees to staff new locations. For
couples who both worked for IBM, it was a lark. For the rest
of us, our husbands couldn't find jobs in Boulder, so we asked
the company for different jobs."

But Westlake's management had made an ef-
fort, explains Jay Allen. In addition to IBM's existing spouse
placement practice, site management contracted with Ca-
reermoves, a division of Homequity, to provide spouse placement assistance which included job information tailored for
the Boulder/Denver labor market. Further, they paid for a
spouse trip for a job search prior to the time it was covered
under IBM's practice.

In the end, for most employees with working spouses it was the depressed state of the Denver/Boulder labor market that determined their decisions.

Despite the criticism, the entire relocation took place with very few employee complaints or appeals—something which surprised management. From the announcement through March 1987, there were only three complaints taken by Westlake employees to higher level executives beyond the site via IBM's open door policy, and complaint or grievance activity within the site was minimal. Letters to the company via its Speak Up programs were also minimal, with only two dealing with move guidelines. This was not sufficient activity to cause the company to alter its move guidelines.

The greatest level of complaints or inquiries occurred after the Greencastle announcement as Westlake employees tried to understand what they viewed as less favorable treatment. That is, IBMers at Westlake who had decided to leave the company wanted the higher level of separation benefits awarded at Greencastle.

Jay Allen commented, "I believe that the emotion surrounding the move really got in the way. Perhaps that should have been anticipated. And this emotion only escalated in November when the Greencastle announcement was made, and in the minds of Westlake's employees, they were treated like second-class citizens. This emotional dynamic is real and had a significant impact."

Don Upton is convinced that many of Westlake's former employees made the wrong decision when they chose not to go to Boulder. "Many didn't want to come with us. It really boiled down to, 'I'm working for IBM because it has a facility in Westlake, California, and that's where I want to be—not in Boulder.' I feel that too many individuals' thought process was based on wanting to live in Southern California rather than thinking about their careers. My vision was and still is that they'd be better off coming with us."

Perhaps Don Upton expected people to be a little more rational in making fundamental decisions about their lives than is realistic. If so, he is like a great many other managers in this regard.

"When I step back and look at my life over the last ten years," an employee told us, "I realize that I handled most of my decisions emotionally even though I thought I was making them objectively. This includes going through a divorce, changing jobs, moving to a new home. These kinds of decisions are the most difficult for people to make. Companies need to keep this in mind."

Summary of Lessons Learned   In moving its Westlake facility to Boulder IBM's managers did many things correctly. Specifically they

■ planned the move with both the schedule of business and the needs of relocating families in mind;

■ considered the probability of each employee individually moving and what would influence him or her positively, and planned accordingly;

■ announced the move to all employees and had managers talk with individual employees about their options;

■ alerted community officials to the move and fitted their package of community actions to the actual setting (in Westlake much less was required than in Greencastle);

■ put in place at Boulder special task forces to help with the relocation to take pressure off the people coming from Westlake; and

■ utilized multiple sources to get new people to staff the organization during and after the move.

The value of these actions was proven by the success of the move itself.

"NOW I'M A 'REDEPLOY' "

Chapter Six

How do individuals deal with change? In our society everything happens so quickly today, and so many things are different. To stay in touch people have to make adjustments continually. If people don't change, they can be left behind.

Some make the decision to try to keep things as they are in their lives. They try to hang on to the same job. They try to remain in the same community. Often they make real sacrifices to avoid change. Good jobs are lost. Better jobs are let go if a big change is required. Often these people wish they could bring themselves to accept change, to do something very different. They look at people who do make big changes and they say, "How do they do it? I wish I could."

The redeployment process at IBM meant that many people had to make decisions about change. Some chose to retire or resign from the company rather than relocate or be retrained. Others chose to take a new assignment and do something very different in their lives.

This chapter is about people who made big changes in their lives. Some had great fear about the future. They didn't know how it would turn out. They sometimes wished the change didn't have to be made, but they summoned up the courage and did their best.

Others greeted change with pleasure. They saw not risk but opportunity. They figured, "What the heck, I'll give it a try. Nothing ventured, nothing gained." Or they said, "After all, that's what life is about. I want a new experience. I want to see if I can advance my career. I want to meet some new people."

The reader will meet both kinds of people in this chapter: both the hesitant and the gung ho.

Four Different Concepts of What Makes a Career   A key element of how people meet change in the workplace involves their conception of a career. Unfortunately, most people and most companies do not think about careers in an imaginative fashion. Because of this people miss opportunities and companies squander talent.

In talking to many people about their careers during the research for this book and for another I have written,[1] I have identified four principal concepts of careers.

The simplest concept is of a career as a single job that a person will do all his or her life. It is probably the most widely held concept and is common among groups as diverse in our work force as blue-collar workers and professionals. Thus a steelworker thinks of his career as the job he is doing in the mill; a clerical worker as her job as a secretary; a policeman as his or her beat; a lawyer as his efforts for his or her clients.

Concept two is of a career as a series of steps up a promotion ladder, ordinarily in the same function. At each level a person has a different job and wider responsibilities, though in essentially the same broad area. This concept is very widespread, especially among managers, administrators, and some professionals.

Concept three involves a career as a sequence of activities of a very different nature. Ordinarily, there is no advancement up a ladder, but instead a series of unrelated jobs which a person may do for variety or because circumstances force him or her into this pattern. A variation of this involves the career as a succession of different projects, usually in the same profession. Thus, the career of a research chemist is comprised by the major projects he or she has worked on; or, of a construction engineer, by the buildings he or she has been involved in. An electronics engineer may think of the different generations of computer technology he or she has helped develop.

---

[1] D. Quinn Mills, *Not Like Our Parents* (New York: William Morrow, 1987).

Concept four adds to the elements of concept three movement up a hierarchy. This is the broadest and most encompassing concept of a career.

A concept four person builds a career from diverse assignments. As different assignments are completed, he or she becomes more knowledgeable and able to do more for the company. But most companies make it surprisingly difficult for people to do very different things, and so force many talented people to go elsewhere for challenge or advancement opportunity.

Old Career Concepts Waste Talent   There are people in our society who are satisfied with concepts one and two. Yet in today's world of rapid change, there is a far greater risk of unemployment if a person holds tightly to these concepts. A person holding tenaciously to a job may find that he or she has been made obsolete by a technical change or increased competition. A person trying to climb a functional ladder may find the number of rungs reduced and the space between rungs increased as the company cuts administrative overhead.

In most companies people want to win promotion competitions. The result is that people climb until they are unhappy in the work that they do. It is not only that people become incompetent—the Peter Principle—but also that they become bored and unhappy.

People can be productive if they enjoy their work, and often they can find enjoyment if given diversity and challenge. The focus of careers ought to be on what people want to do, so that they don't compete for a job, obtain it, and then find that they don't like it.

As people remain healthier for many more years during their lives and are willing to work longer, concepts one and two become increasing liabilities. Instead, what is important is that people be able to fashion a sequence of assignments which satisfies them.

For some people diversity is sufficient reward in itself and they are satisfied with a concept three career. By embracing learning and diversity these people are insulated psychologically against obsolence; and by being satisfied at whatever levels they attain, they escape the potential disappointment of failure to advance up a corporate ladder.

Many ambitious people go through an evolution in their lives from an aspiration for a concept four career when they are young, to a concept three career when opportunities are blocked for advancement. They are fortunate to be able to switch their aspirations, rather than be plateaued and increasingly bored in a single job or function for the remainder of their working lives.

The satisfaction of people in their jobs and the performance of people in our companies would both be enhanced if individuals and companies began to see concepts three and four as the proper concept of a person's career and abandoned concepts one and two as outdated and hazardous to both individuals and companies.

Few companies invest enough effort in retraining and relocating people to build and reinforce concepts three and four in the thinking of their employees. Yet there is evidence from a variety of sources that people are more flexible and capable than ordinarily thought, and so can make a concept three or four career a reality.

One surprising source of evidence is from the experience of managers and professionals released from their companies and given to outplacement firms for assistance in obtaining new jobs. In most instances these people have gotten better jobs—in terms of pay and level—than those from which they were laid off.

I was reluctant to believe this, since it suggests that people could better their positions if they would look outside the company for new places on their own initiative, rather than wait to be laid off. Yet apparently this is exactly the case. Most companies give employees so little opportunity to transfer and renew themselves in a different setting that those individuals who are forced to do so often find new productivity elsewhere.

Probably this conclusion is only valid for an expanding economy where jobs are available, and for people who have had help in preparing themselves for a major change. But for those who get such help, careers can be advanced even by an involuntary release from their present occupation.

Many people are so reluctant to change that they fail to seek out opportunities for better positions, both within and outside a company.

In the future people will have to be increasingly adaptable, accept retraining, and change careers if they wish to keep up in the economy. Some refer to this as a need for multiple careers, but it is better understood as a concept four career. This is because people then understand that what is happening to them is not unusual, and does not represent the failure of one career effort and start of another, but instead is a normal part of the development of a modern career. They are not people to be sympathized with but instead to be envied, for they are at the forefront of change and adaptation.

"Change is built on interaction," Jack Stillens told us. This is true not only of careers but in the products a business sells and the methods it uses. A company with many concept four people who move frequently and across major lines in the company finds itself with people who through continual interaction with others are well adapted to change in all aspects of their activities at the company. People who fear to change their jobs also fear change in how they do those jobs and in how the company does its business.

It follows that a company should recognize the modern shape of careers and try to develop opportunities for people inside, while simultaneously building loyalty to keep people from going to other companies. IBM does both, and by so doing gets the maximum benefit from the abilities of its people.

An executive's career at IBM often entails moving between line and staff positions in a sort of cycle. For example, many managers are given an opportunity at some point in their career to spend two years in a staff assignment at corporate headquarters. This enables them to learn about how the company runs from the top. It is usually a very positive experience because there is lots of action at the corporate level.

Ken Taylor had such an assignment. He joined IBM as a marketing representative in September 1966. For twelve years he sold medical equipment, concluding as national sales manager. But in January 1984, IBM sold the business and Ken took a marketing staff job elsewhere in the company. A year later he accepted a two-year tour at corporate headquarters helping to run the management training and development activities.

As his stint in Armonk ended, Ken's wife was expecting twins and they chose to go to California, where her parents lived. He applied for a job there with Rolm Corporation, which IBM had just acquired. He interviewed for a position on the Rolm sales division staff in Santa Clara. To get the job he told the person who would be his boss, "I have worked in sales and sales management and I know the corporate world from being in Armonk."

His boss-to-be hesitated not an instant, as Ken recalls it, before saying, "You're hired."

Concept four is a way of life in IBM. How has it worked in people's lives? How do such people feel about their lives? What are the costs of a concept four career and what are its characteristics? What is the behavior of people which makes it possible?

Concept Four in Action   Most of those who took redeployment at IBM were concept four people. They took new jobs in the redeployment effort because they wanted to take their careers in a different direction. Redeployment is not temporary, it should be emphasized. The new assignments are permanent until the person makes another career move. Despite its large size and formality, the company does not try to predetermine a person's career. People look for opportunities, receive advice, and take on new challenges, all the while shaping a personal career through a succession of positions.

Here are the stories of several individuals who used the redeployment and remissioning as opportunities to advance their careers in unusual directions.

The Importance of Choice   Ted Tsutsui, formerly a senior design specialist at San Jose and now training to be a programmer, is a person who welcomes change. "Most people don't like change unless they are unhappy where they are," Ted said. "Not me. To me change is exciting. I learn something new. It revitalizes my life. But I don't know if I'd like to be relocating. It takes a special kind of individual to do that.

"My shift to programming has been a benefit to me and to the company. I looked to see how it would benefit me first. I decided that if the company is willing to educate me, what do I have to lose? Sure, I've got to put out more effort, but sometimes that's good for me. I went through two classes with twenty-five other people. We got to be a close-knit group. We cared about each other—like a family.

"The most important thing about the redeployment effort is that individuals have a choice. It makes no sense to send someone who hasn't made the choice that it's what he or she wants to do to a different job."

George Krawiec, who helped manage the redeployment effort from corporate headquarters, also understood this. "People are excited about the opportunities that redeployment offers because they are not forced to do it. They are asked if they want to do something different." That is, redeployment is another option for advancing one's career in IBM, and people who take it do so because it fits into their concept of a career.

"The Company Allows Me to Be Me"   Ron Sprinkle has a pair of the bluest eyes in creation. Set in a round, healthy face, they give him an expression of openness and honesty. He has been twenty years with IBM and by virtue of the remissioning of Boulder has just made the transition from blue-collar to white-collar work.

Ron started with IBM in Lexington, Kentucky, where he was employed in the production of typewriter ribbons. After several years that technology declined, and he moved into magnetic media. Mag med, as it was called, had an even shorter lifespan at Lexington. When its production was discontinued, Ron went into plastics.

After fifteen years at the Lexington facility, his manager told the people who reported to him, Ron included, that IBM had opportunities in plastics work in the manufacturing plant at Boulder. At the time Ron had three daughters, the eldest of whom was eight. He and his wife saw this as an opportunity to see the rest of the country. IBM flew him to Boulder to try out the job for a week. He knew he did not have to relocate, since others in the Lexington plant had less service with the company than he, and IBM ordinarily relied on lesser service employees to fill openings elsewhere if more senior employees were not interested.

But Ron enjoyed the work at Boulder and he and his wife both wanted a change of scene; so he accepted the job at Boulder.

Five years later the company announced that it was going to move manufacturing from Boulder, so that again Ron had to adjust his career to the changing needs of the business. Service repair positions were being increased in number at Boulder, and since Ron and his family wanted to remain in the Boulder area, he applied for one. Accepted, he was sent to Atlanta for three months training—the first prolonged separation he had had from his family.

After twenty years in manufacturing Ron had attained a high classification level and a good salary. The service repair job carried a lower level and less pay, so that after a period of time if he did not move up the new ladder on to which he had stepped, he would have to accept a reduction in pay. But service repair was growing in IBM and at Boulder, and he saw an opportunity to move to higher levels in his new area.

Ron knew that he was very lucky. He was a manufacturing production worker in a company that was experiencing weak market demand, and so was overstaffed in manufacturing. Not only that, but the location at which he worked was being phased out as a manufacturing center. In most other American companies, despite his twenty years of service, he would have been a shoe-in for layoff. But Ron wasn't worrying about being laid off. Instead he had just completed a lengthy training course, was moving into a white-collar occupation with considerable potential for advancement, and had been able to make the transition without unemployment or the need to relocate his family. Rather than dreading the business downturn for his company and despairing for his own future, Ron was embarked on an exciting change in career. "Now I'm a 'redeploy,' " he said.

Although out of the factory only a short period, Ron already thought of himself as in the mainstream of the technicians' world in high tech. If he chose to remain in service repair, he had his eye on a position as a manager of customer contacts. But that was not the only opportunity open to him. He had been informed by his manager that the company had positions available in systems engineering, and he was considering whether or not to apply for one. If he were to enter systems engineering, however, he thought he might have to relocate, and so was considering that option with his family.

These are hard times in Colorado. The state's unemployment rate is about 9 percent, and many of Ron's neighbors are out of work. He is acutely aware of the advantages of his own position, even though his own company has had its difficulty in the marketplace also. "This company has been very good to me," he said. "It allows me to be me."

"Each Position Prepares Me for the Future"   Ruthanne Ketcham is a person for whom change is a significant element in building her career.

Following college she worked for several small consulting companies, then for Citicorp starting a new business. From Citicorp she went to General Foods to get more direct experience in marketing, and thence to Harvard Business School to get an MBA.

Because at the school she felt very comfortable with computers, she sought an interview with an IBM manager who came to the campus. "He explained to me what he did," she said, "and then told me that he didn't have a specific job he wanted to fill, but that he needed some new ideas in marketing techniques." She got the job.

After working in product marketing at division headquarters for two years, her manager told her she ought to move into IBM's large systems group, where there was enhanced opportunity for personal growth and advancement.

When the redeployment initiative came along, she applied for a line position in sales. She was "somewhat apprehensive" about moving from a headquarters position to one in the line, and from salary to part salary (65 percent) and the remainder commission. To reassure herself of the wisdom of the move, she asked each of her managers (at the company's different levels) whether or not she should make the change. All encouraged her to do so. They were right. A year later, she made IBM's Golden Circle of the top marketing representatives.

One man she met at her sales training class impressed her and gave her confidence, because she saw that her concerns were shared by others. He was very nervous about his first class, which involved a customer-tailored sales call. "He had fought in Vietnam," she said, "and he said to me, 'I remember how scared I was learning how to fly a helicopter. But now I say to myself that if I could learn to fly a helicopter, then I can learn to be a marketing rep.' "

Now finished with her sales training she commented, "With each position I prepare myself for the future. Unlike other companies, many career paths are available. There is no typical career path in IBM.

"I never saw redeployment as anything but an opportunity to be on a faster career path. I have never felt that I have been forced into this. There's always something else I can do. Of the other things I could have done, this was the best opportunity. I think that if I'm willing to accept change and participate in change, then I'll always do well."

A Skiing Cowboy   Dick Jacquemard sat in his office dressed in a blue suit, white shirt, and crimson tie dotted with light blue and gray rosettes. He was slender and tanned, looking much younger than his fifty-five years. On his feet were well-worn cowboy boots of top-quality leather, decorated with elaborate stitching. His thoughts wandered toward his small ranch, almost visible from the Boulder facility, and to the horses now grazing in the paddocks behind his house. He was eager to leave work and ride under the afternoon's clear skies.

Dick's mind was very much relieved this day. For weeks he had been gearing himself to accept another assignment from the company. He was going, he had decided, to Charlotte, North Carolina, to which the production of copiers and printers was being transferred. A senior manager in the manufacturing unit, he was much needed in the transfer process.

But he very much wanted not to go. He had come to Boulder twenty years ago, not expecting to stay more than two years. At the time he had been in the personnel function, and his impression was that IBM didn't want personnel managers in manufacturing to remain more than a couple of years at the same site. But he had fallen in love with Colorado, and he had five children attending the local schools. So he had tried to remain in Colorado.

Thirty years ago Dick had joined IBM in Poughkeepsie, New York, in a manufacturing facility. He spent six months on assignment to each functional area (production, engineering, shipping, and personnel), and ended up staying in personnel. Following Poughkeepsie he had an assignment of several years to corporate headquarters in Armonk, also in personnel; then was asked to go to Boulder. It was 1967. Despite IBM's proclivity for relocating managers, Dick had remained for twenty years in Colorado.

For eight years he served as the chief personnel officer in the manufacturing unit at Boulder. This was substantially longer than the expected assignment, and he had several times been offered other positions. But he had first one, then another, then yet other children in high school, and there was never a time that was convenient for the family to relocate. He had purchased some land and enjoyed riding horses. And in the winter the family found time to ski. Soon Dick became an accomplished skier himself and became involved in ski patrol activities.

By 1976 Dick realized that he could no longer remain at Boulder in the personnel function. As a high-level manager he knew the company and its systems, and had the managerial skills to serve in other functions. He had never really been involved as a manager in the production aspect of manufacturing, except for six months of exposure early in his career at Poughkeepsie, but he had the managerial skills to be a line manager. He applied for a transfer to one of the top production management positions at Boulder, was selected by the plant's manufacturing manager, and started a new phase of his career in production.

For ten years now he had served in the production of copiers and printers. He had seen the products improve greatly in quality and in market acceptance. But he had also known of the difficulties in being profitable at the available sales volume, and was not surprised when the corporation decided to consolidate production into other IBM plants. It made sense for production to leave Colorado, but as for himself, he did not want to go with it.

Very soon after the announcement of the remissioning of the Boulder facility, Dick was asked by his boss to accompany the production operation to Charlotte.

Dick declined. Instead, he prepared himself to look for a new assignment in Boulder, as so many of his fellow employees at the plant were doing. He told his manager that he wanted to be redeployed at Boulder.

Several weeks later his manager again approached him about going to Charlotte. His knowledge of the production process and the plastics involved was important to the successful transfer, his boss told him. Still, Dick didn't want to leave, and again declined to go.

A few months passed, and Dick had not yet found a new area to go into at the remissioned facility. Again his boss approached him about going to Charlotte. The repeated, low-key effort of the company, acting through his manager, to get him to relocate was having its impact on Dick's resolve. If they persisted, he realized, there was probably a real need. And he knew that for years he had relocated to a lesser degree than his peers in IBM. His basic loyalty to the company began to assert itself. The company had done a great deal for him, and if it now needed his support in return, he was prepared to put aside his own convenience and do what they asked.

Dick accepted an offer to visit Charlotte. He found it a pleasant community. Soon thereafter he agreed to leave Colorado and go to North Carolina. Another trip resulted in his selection of a building site for his new home. By late 1986 construction was under way on the house, and in the spring of 1987 the building was almost complete.

Although still reluctant to leave Colorado, Dick felt that he had done the right thing in agreeing to go with the company. He had other business opportunities in Colorado, but to have simply quit IBM would have been to lose some of his rapidly accumulating pension benefits, now that he had long service, and to betray the company.

Then early in 1987, as his house in Charlotte was nearing completion, the company announced an early retirement package. An employee with a certain number of years of service could add five years to his or her age and five years to his or her length of service in computing the pension benefit due. For Dick, with almost thirty years of service, the result was very attractive. By retiring he could stay in Colorado.

But would his boss let him retire? The company would still need him in Charlotte.

When Dick told his boss about his decision to retire, his boss did not object. The corporation had offered the early retirement plan, and Dick had every right to accept it if he so desired. Copier production would have to get started in Charlotte without Dick.

Delighted, Dick quickly sold his new house in North Carolina. Just as quickly he purchased a duplex at a ski area in the Rockies. His new career was taking shape. He would run the ski patrol at the mountain and rent property which he would slowly accumulate.

Now as he sat at his desk he was only a few workdays away from retirement. His horses awaited him, and his skis. He was leaving one career for another, but he was going to remain where his heart would always be: in Colorado.

Into International Trade from Middle America   Sandy August began her work career at a large aerospace firm as a buyer of materials and looked forward to a series of promotions. But she knew of the ups and downs of the aerospace business. Seeking greater economic security because of her two young children, she applied to IBM for a position. She was prepared to take a step down the ladder if necessary, and when IBM offered her a position as a secretary, and one of the first people to be hired at the then new Boulder facility, she accepted it. That was twenty-two years ago.

In the ensuing years Sandy moved into professional positions in personnel, education and training, and finally into management development for IBM at the Boulder facility. In the process she became a first-level manager, and became familiar with IBM's hiring process.

"IBM should never hire a person who hasn't worked for another company first," Sandy insists, "because if they haven't been elsewhere, as I was, they take IBM for granted and the company doesn't get the loyalty it deserves."

Although she had made progress in her career, it was not as rapid as it might have been. Sandy was continually turning down opportunities to take transfers or promotions within IBM and even within the Boulder facility. She had two small children and wanted to have as much time with them as possible. Never did she see any signs that her reluctance to take more responsibility had been held against her in the company.

But now her children were older. No longer was she needed by them as she had been earlier. Her thoughts now turned to her own career. When Boulder was remissioned, she recognized that new opportunities would be presented.

In Poughkeepsie, New York, IBM had an organization which procured supplies and materials from IBM subsidiaries abroad for IBM facilities in the United States. Although it seemed logical that a unit engaged in international trade would be located on the Atlantic coast, it was not necessary, and IBM took advantage of the physical space and people made available in Boulder by the termination of manufacturing there to move the international distribution unit to Boulder.

One day Sandy's Boulder manager, who had been transferred to the international unit, came to her boss, and then to her, offering a position in the new unit. The job looked very interesting—an opportunity to communicate with people all over the globe and to learn about other lands. She was offered the management of a unit of nine persons, and accepted with excitement. For Sandy, the remissioning of Boulder was an opportunity to see the world.

The Worried and the Gung Ho   Although concept four people are willing to take their careers in very different directions as the opportunity arises, they differ considerably in how they feel about each change. Some are enthusiastic, gung ho. Others are hesitant and fearful. And the exact combination differs for each individual. Ted Tsutsui welcomed a new position, but didn't want to relocate. Ruthanne Ketcham was quite prepared to relocate, but was nervous about going on commission.

At first, often there is surprise. In today's fast-paced world, people suddenly discover that things are not as stable as they thought. Sometimes the revelation comes in an unusual and dramatic fashion.

"Oh My God! This Is Really Serious!"   Doug Norton graduated from college with an engineering degree in May 1985, and soon after joined IBM. He was assigned to a lab and loved the work.

"I hadn't been with IBM for a year when we began to have career awareness meetings as part of the re-deployment initiative," he said. "I sat out a couple, then went to one concerning opportunities in other areas of IBM. I looked around at the meeting and saw that my own manager was there, looking for somewhere else to go. I said to myself, 'Oh my God, this is really serious!' "

He applied for a sales job and got two offers. One of the offers was described to him as follows: "We'll give you as much rope as you want. If you can't handle it, we'll pull it back. But feel free to take as much as you can handle."

"I liked that," Doug told us. "So I took that offer and moved from Lexington, Kentucky, to Los Angeles."

Herb Underwood commented, "It's not just IBM but the entire industry that is discovering and becoming more proficient in the uses of automation. It is changing so quickly that we are constantly retraining, reeducating to keep up with it. Before I was involved in automation, I was a circuit-card tester, and then I heard about the robotic school and went to my manager. I talked to him and found out some information and decided that it sounded real exciting, and I went into it and wouldn't trade it for anything in the world."

Concept four people do unusual things in fashioning their careers. At IBM many managers left their supervisory jobs and went into training for field service jobs. They saw an opportunity in what concept one people would have viewed as an inconvenient change and concept two people would have viewed as stepping down. For example, Garo Agopian, a manager in the San Jose development lab, said, "I was an engineer for about a year and then I was a manager the last four years that I spent in San Jose. About a year ago when this opportunity came up, my manager knew that I was gone! This is really a great opportunity for me. I've been looking forward to this, and I just grabbed the opportunity and jumped on it."

Jennifer Poe came to IBM to do something different than the job for which she was hired. "I came to IBM two years ago as a secretary," she explained, "hoping to work into a programming field." She knew that such shifts in position were possible at IBM. "I was lucky enough to come across a transition training program a year later," she said, when the company needed programmers. "I went into the training program and had probably the most exciting, frustrating, gratifying fifteen weeks you could have."

Doug, Herb, Garo, and Jennifer were enthusiastic. Greg Dietzel was apprehensive. "A change definitely makes you nervous when you first start out," he said. "I came from the plant and I had a lot of confidence, and I thought I could do the job, but I was sort of hedging my bets. So I came out as a systems engineer and after being in the field for a couple of months and going to a couple of the classes, I said, 'Hey, I can do this.' So I switched over and now I'm going to be a marketing rep."

David Kennedy, whom the reader will recall was site manager at Greencastle, summed up the perspective of the concept four person and the company which relies on such people in the following comment about his various assignments: "I've never been completely qualified for any job I've had at IBM. I'm learning another piece of the business now that Greencastle is closed. At IBM, they always believe in giving you a full plate."

A *S*tep *B*ackward *B*efore *S*teps *F*orward   On August 3, 1981, Bob Bailey was on strike. For four years he had been an air traffic controller working for the Federal Aviation Administration at the Denver Center, located north of Denver at Longmont, Colorado. From Denver Center air traffic controllers directed all en route flights going coast to coast and north and south over nine states. Even at night the skies were crowded with transcontinental flights. "I really enjoyed the challenge of juggling all those planes," Bob said.

Yet there were problems. Bob worked a rotating shift which often brought him into the center late at night, and sometimes required him to be back early the next day. Often he would work the 6:00 A.M. to 2:00 P.M. shift only to come back in at 11:00 P.M. "There wasn't time to adjust between working periods," he said. "The FAA would fix the computers on the night shift, so when the controllers really needed the computers, they were unavailable. When the controllers most needed management understanding, there was none. The FAA was contradictory. They required the controllers to make decisions, but treated us like children." Bob became increasingly angry with the unwillingness of the FAA to adjust the schedule, provide computer support, or improve supervision. He had learned air traffic control in the Air Force and resented what he felt was a patronizing attitude from FAA management toward him and his fellow workers.

Like most air traffic controllers, Bob was a member of the Professional Air Traffic Controllers' Organization (PATCO). When in late July 1981, PATCO called a strike against the FAA, an agency of the federal government, in violation of the law, Bob and some twelve thousand other controllers walked off the job. So uniform among controllers was the strike that when President Reagan announced on August 3 that all controllers who did not return to work would be dismissed, Bob was convinced that even should the president dismiss him and his fellows they would soon be recalled to work.

Thus it came about that on August 3 Bob was

fired from his job as an air traffic controller. Initially he attended meetings with other controllers and waited to be recalled to work. But days passed into weeks and weeks into months without the government settling the strike with PATCO. Some few controllers returned to their jobs, but most of the strikers remained out and lost their jobs. Meanwhile, the FAA was hiring replacements for those who had been fired. Since the job was well-paying, the openings were being filled. It began to seem likely that strikers would have a long wait before being rehired.

Still, the strikers were convinced that the nation's air traffic control system could not be run successfully without them. So they sought ways to make do until the government reached an agreement with their union and returned them to their jobs.

Bob began to take odd jobs in gasoline stations and retail stores. He earned very little by the standard of his pay as an air traffic controller. But he was single and was able to get by with little pay. As the months dragged on the FAA showed itself able to operate the air system with supervisors, assignees from the military, and with newly hired replacements for the strikers. Slowly it dawned on Bob and his fellow strikers that their years as air traffic controllers were over. There was no substantial market for air traffic controllers other than the FAA or the military, so that he realized that his once valuable skills were now of no value at all. It was the end of a promising career; a trip from high on the nation's ladder of occupations and salaries to near its bottom.

What was Bob to do now? His skills as an air traffic controller were of little or no use except to the government, from which he was now estranged. The world as he had known it had collapsed. Always a government employee, first in the military, then in the FAA, he was now on his own in the private sector. In his mid-thirties, with skills he could not use, he had a living standard he could no longer afford. What stretched ahead of him were years of difficulty and privation. Yet, refusing to give in to despair, Bob began to look for a new career.

Many of Bob's neighbors in Longmont worked at IBM's Boulder facility. From them he had heard that the company was a good employer and that it was hiring people for temporary factory jobs. So late in 1982 Bob applied for a job at the company's Boulder complex. Having few, if any, skills directly applicable to IBM's business, Bob asked for a largely unskilled job in the factory. He sought work as an assembler of electronic equipment or as a shipping clerk in the warehouse.

In his interviews Bob told each manager who might be his boss that he had been an air traffic controller and that he had been dismissed for participating in the strike. "They seemed to think that my previous job, with its high requirements for mental concentration, gave me an extra dimension which might be useful in an employee. They seemed to think of me as a resource who could contribute a lot to the company. They knew I had exercised a lot of responsibility and decision-making at the FAA. Also, IBM managers seemed to pay a lot of attention to attitude. They wanted someone who supports the company and wants to get ahead."

So IBM hired Bob as a forklift driver in the Boulder warehouse on a temporary basis. After six months Bob's tour as a temporary expired and he was let go by IBM. Soon he found a similar job on a full-time basis at Storage Technology, the largest employer in the area and a company largely founded by former IBM executives. But Bob found Storage a less desirable employer than IBM and kept alive his application for a full-time position at IBM. And in the spring of 1983 IBM wrote to him offering a full-time position as a forklift driver in the Boulder warehouse.

Despite being a company in which there is no union representation in the United States, and despite a well-known preference to stay that way, Bob felt no prejudice against him by IBM due to his participation in the PATCO strike. In fact, to his knowledge, IBM hired eight other former PATCO strikers at Boulder in the same time period, three of whom by mid-1987 were supervisors for IBM.

Why had he been so persistent in seeking a floor-level factory position at IBM? Bob's answer was simple: "I wanted to get my foot in the door. I had been told by my neighbors who work for IBM that the company would recognize initiative and ability. That I'd get ahead if I worked hard. I was starting at the bottom again in my mid-thirties. I was going to be earning about one-third what I had been earning at the FAA. I had to try to find a company where if I worked hard, I could get ahead."

Bob went to work on the loading dock for a forty-hour week. Quickly his manager saw in Bob a resource, and allowed him to begin to oversee the dock on the second shift. Word got around that if there was a problem, go see Bob Bailey.

In mid-1984 Bob learned of an opening in the computer room as a computer operator. This was more directly in the line of growing activities in IBM, and offered the possibility of further advances. He talked to the manager in the computer room, and after a period of some months, since his own boss didn't want to lose him on the dock, Bob went to work in the computer room as the result of a lateral transfer.

In the late fall of 1985, the company publicized internally that it had an acute shortage of systems programmers. Anyone interested in training for such a position was to notify his or her manager and submit an application. Some one thousand people applied at Boulder, including Bob. After programming aptitude tests, one hundred were selected for interviews. From the interviews forty emerged as selected to enter the programming course. Bob was one of them. On

February 1, 1986, the programming class began—fifteen weeks of forty hours per week classroom instruction, followed by months of on-the-job applications. In late spring of 1987, Bob received his associate programming certificate and his first substantial advance in level and compensation since joining IBM.

In his four years at IBM, Bob had initiated three lateral transfers and a major training effort. Initially, he brought to the factory and its loading docks a substantial degree of effort and imagination and willingness to accept responsibility. But he did not see the manufacturing plant as a growing area of the business, nor as one requiring sufficiently high skills on which to build a career. As a result he, and according to him others in the factory as well, welcomed the transition of Boulder from a manufacturing facility to a programming center.

To take advantage of the coming opportunity, Bob found a way into the computer room and thence into programming. Now firmly established on the lower rung of the programming ladder, he sees the remissioning of the Boulder facility as a great personal opportunity. "The corporation predicts that Boulder will be the largest computing center in the world by 1990," he said. "Already the computer center here is the largest in Colorado."

Like other concept four people, Bob was willing to take a step or two down and backward, as he did when he lost his job as an air traffic controller, to open up new opportunities in his career, as he did when he went to IBM and began to look for opportunities to move up.

A More **R**elaxed **L**ife   Forging a concept four career is not always a succession of more and more challenging assignments. Sometimes a person needs to take some time out to let the dust settle. Not infrequently people have personal problems and need to do something different for that reason. Several people we interviewed found IBM surprisingly willing to accommodate their needs. The company was flexible enough to adjust to change in its employees' lives and was prepared to do so to help its employees keep their personal lives intact as well as their professional lives.

"Help Me Out of This Mess"   "I was living in upstate New York," Bernie Nathan told us, "and had been divorced from my wife. She was so upset about the situation that she wrote a letter to Frank Cary, then IBM's chairman. She accused me of forging her name on stock certificates, using the WATTS telephone line for personal calls, and other things.

"The letter went back from Cary's office to management at my facility. The site manager called me in and said, 'Here's what she wrote.' It was the first I knew about the letter. He went through the letter point by point and asked me about each one. I dealt with it honestly, even where I looked bad.

"After we went through every point, I asked, 'Am I fired?'

"They said, 'No, you have explained what *actually* happened.'

"I asked if they could help me out of this messy situation by transferring me. Within two weeks I had a job with IBM in Virginia. You don't hate a company that treats you that way.

"I know many people think of IBM as a monolithic company, but I think of it as a beehive with various honeycombs. I've never felt like a number in this company. They've respected me."

Nor was this the end of relocations for Bernie. In 1986 he was working in IBM's semiconductor manufacturing plant in Burlington, Vermont. He saw on the bulletin board that the company was looking for volunteers to go into marketing.

He wanted a change, and so he applied. He was in a staff function and Burlington needed to cut costs. "My manager told me that if that's what I wanted to do, do it."

So Bernie went to California to become a salesperson. "You have to understand that this is like going from a rowing team to a track team. For twenty years my world was semiconductors. Now I act as a consultant to a customer. That's difficult especially when you don't know anything about the equipment. I didn't even understand the sales and hardware language. I had to work to understand.

"What is most dramatic is the willingness of the company to move me across the continent to my new career. They saw themselves as unable to use my talents in Burlington. Now I make money for the company in this job. They take good people and put them in positions where they can make the company money.

"Why not just throw me out the door?" Bernie asked himself rhetorically. "Because I have decades of experience with the company. I know how to get things done. I've been a manager so I'm not hesitant to push when it's necessary. They had an asset in me and were willing to do any reformatting which was necessary for me to be effective.

"In Burlington I never had a white shirt. Headquarters and marketing wear white shirts. But when I came here to sales I knew it was a new game, so I went out and bought white shirts."

"I Needed a Break"   Gale Nelson's parents worked for IBM at the Boulder facility, and as a college student she worked at the plant as a temporary employee. She took her degree in psychology, then entered the Navy. Finishing Officers' Candidate School, she decided not to take a commission, and in 1977 was hired by IBM at Boulder as a permanent employee in manufacturing.

She worked her way up. After three years she attained a management position. After eighteen months as a manager she was responsible for three departments in the assembly area.

Then she found a substantial challenge in bringing to final production a new laser printer. This was a very intense job, involving great personal stress.

As bad luck would have it, this was also a time of great stress in her personal life. She went through a divorce and kept custody of her two small children.

"I needed a break," she said. "I was exhausted."

She talked with her manager about the situation and they worked out an arrangement by which she worked for the United Way for four months before returning to her work in the company. Her personal crisis was relieved, and she was ready to put her full attention back on the company's needs.

"I wanted to manage and to keep growing and moving," she said. "But to progress, I felt that I needed a technical skill."

Hence, when she heard of increased programming opportunities in Boulder, she applied for the programming class. This was just before the remissioning of Boulder was announced.

"There were over three hundred people applying for that class," Gale said. "This was rare to have programming jobs at the Boulder site." When the remissioning was announced people in the programming class were immediately aware that their initiative in learning programming would now pay off in substantial opportunities to use their new skills at Boulder.

Nonetheless, for the time being, Gale has taken a step backward. Her programming position carries less responsibility than her previous manufacturing management job. She is allowed to retain her old salary for several years, but then will either have to have regained her old level or take a pay cut.

She is not dismayed at the prospect. "I need challenge," she said. "The rewards are recognition, growth, and accomplishment. I do a good job because I want to. Then I feel good about myself and that affects my personal life positively.

"This recent change involves learning a new skill, and that is difficult, but my stress was so high in my job before that it seems easy. Now I'm not a manager and I don't have to worry about other people. Because I have less responsibility at work I can put more time into my family.

"It may seem pretty crazy from a business point of view to let a manager like me be retrained to be a programmer," Gale concluded. "But if IBM gets an employee who will go the extra mile for the company, then in the end both the company and the employee win."

Neither Bernie's nor Gale's career was damaged by the changes they requested for personal reasons. And both gained by the experience in the positions to which they were transferred, so that later they were each willing to volunteer for redeployment. The company, at a critical time in their lives, had allowed them to be more relaxed than they could have been otherwise; and their concept of a career had permitted them to make necessary changes without feeling that they had sacrificed their futures.

As a result of its ability to redeploy people, the next business transition—perhaps back to manufacturing from service—will find IBM in a good position.

Summary of Lessons Learned

■ People and companies both need to learn to deal more effectively with change. A company needs to create an environment that allows people to adapt and grow. And people need to learn how to use change to keep themselves up-to-date professionally and, when necessary, to resolve problems in their personal lives.

■ Most companies need for employees to modernize their skills and to work in a more productive way. When an employee wants to do something different at work—for whatever reason, including ambition, personal difficulties, boredom—an opportunity is created for the company.

■ A business slowdown can create opportunity for people, not just fear and insecurity. A person facing a major change may be very afraid of it, but once it is accomplished he or she usually feels fabulous about it, because risks were taken and change allowed to happen. The enthusiasm of many people in the redeployment effort at IBM comes from making a difficult decision and coming out successfully. People are happy not just because of having a new job, but because of great pleasure in themselves. Once a person has done something like this he or she has more self-confidence and can do it again if necessary.

■ People generally are much more flexible than their employers believe, and giving them opportunities to do different things can elicit a very positive and productive response. The employees a company has are a resource, even in bad times, because they can do a variety of things.

■ A company can gain by retraining and redeploying its people from a weak business area to a stronger one, rather than laying some off and hiring others from the outside, because current employees already know the company. If a firm has a strong culture and the right business practices, then it is cheaper to redeploy people who already are adept in the culture and practices than to hire new people and train them about how to do things in the company. If a company lacks a strong culture and appropriate business practices, then it needs a lot more help than just the question of whether to hire or transfer.

HOW TO MANAGE
FOR FULL EMPLOYMENT

Part 1. Top-Level
Commitment

Chapter Seven

I have heard executives in many companies complain that despite considerable effort, they are unable to get most people in their organizations to follow corporate policies or to take actions that will permit the corporation to grow without undue risk. There is too little commitment of lower-level people to corporate goals. This is true of small companies as well as large ones. For many companies the inability to get things done well stands as an insurmountable barrier to expansion.

In contrast, IBM is at its best in getting corporate policies executed down the line. It is said that implementation is 85 percent of making a corporate strategy successful. IBM is expert at implementation.

The company employs some four hundred thousand people worldwide, yet first-level managers seem to know corporate intentions and are willing and able to carry them out. IBM's execution of its business policies is exemplary. Where there are errors, they are more likely those of business strategy than of execution, and this is very unusual among companies. We saw at Boulder, Greencastle, and Westlake that corporate desires were carried out well, despite the enormous size of the company and its employee population.

As I interviewed IBM managers, I was surprised that each person thought that he or she was the key person deciding what should be done and in getting things achieved. Yet to a large degree, corporate-level executives are pulling the strings—directing the show and yet getting people to feel like they're doing it. The company intentionally helped employees to perceive redeployment as a career advance; and our survey of IBMers showed that 70 percent of redeploys did so.

This is a real accomplishment. It is the secret of the company's ability to implement. How does IBM do it? The recipe is complex and has surprising ingredients. Eight factors were critical to the success of the company's redeployment effort:

1. top management focus.
2. establishment of a management process, including staff in a position of authority.
3. a focus on the individual with teamwork also.
4. getting different corporation functions and divisions to work together.
5. establishment of a communications program.
6. establishment of a retraining and education program.
7. line management buy-in.
8. employee cooperation and commitment.

Preceding chapters have told elements of the story of IBM's effort to reorient its people and its facilities during the business downturn of 1985–87. A series of significant lessons emerged about human beings and the managers for whom they work. This chapter brings together the major themes from the experiences recounted in earlier chapters into a plan of action for a company. It shows how IBM managed the overall process of which the events described above are elements. The company uses these practices to manage a very large organization, but they are as easily utilized in smaller settings. The action plan below can be used by any company and for many purposes. It is not limited to employment security.

As preceding chapters have demonstrated, IBM now resorts to redeployment and remissioning as methods of maintaining full employment when business declines. How did IBM get into these practices? The answer is instructive, because it was not through having to deal with business downturns, but rather through coping with explosive growth.

Remissioning, retraining, and redeployment are not mechanisms designed solely for periods of poor business. Instead, they are techniques IBM developed in part to cope with its long periods of rapid growth. During these periods the employee population expanded steadily. The company was continually promoting and reassigning people as it grew. Yet fundamental to its management style was a culture which had to be transmitted to new IBMers. Rapid growth made it more important to transmit the culture via changing assignments for people than to hire in from the outside in order to attain particular skills. Hence, the company developed a practice of flexibility in assignments, retraining, and promotions from within.

When business downturns occurred, the company adapted its methods to protect the employment of people. But as downturns have become more frequent and more severe, the company has developed other techniques to balance its human resources and thereby keep new hiring to a minimum. These techniques are the essence of resource balancing.

Top Management Focus   Top managers play a key role in influencing what activities are given high priority by others in the organization. IBM's top management has created mechanisms by which it expresses its own priorities and continually reinforces the message. These mechanisms are described in this chapter.

In order to make employment security a reality, IBM must do many things that other companies don't do. It must balance its resources so that work-force surpluses do not develop that cannot be handled except by layoffs. If this is not done, providing employment security becomes prohibitively expensive, even for IBM. Ensuring that the company takes the actions necessary to make the full employment practice a reality is the special responsibility of top management.

A look at the organization chart of IBM tells much more about how the company is actually managed than can ordinarily be gleaned from the typical organization chart of a corporation. IBM's chart shows not only boxes representing operating divisions and staff units, each reporting to some higher level, but also indicates certain key committees which meet regularly and play an important role in the management of the company.

Why do IBM's top executives get together regularly? The committees serve several purposes. They permit extensive exchange of information among top executives about the business; they allow executives to comment on significant issues that arise; and they contribute to the judgment exercised by the executives who make key decisions. The committees also play a significant role in making full employment happen.

Earlier organization charts do not make the role of the committees so apparent. In fact, many charts were drawn without the committees appearing on them. Until the late 1950s the committees did not exist. At that time the company commissioned what was the first and only full-scale outside evaluation of its management structure, conducted by a large consulting company. Responding to the consultant's report, IBM's CEO decided that the company had become too large for him to run by himself, and established a top-level management committee to assist him. The idea was simply that several heads were better than one in thinking about what ought to be done.

As the company has continued to grow, it has attempted to delegate operational decisions further down the managerial ladder. That effort continues today. Yet by the standards of most very large companies, IBM continues to be a very much centrally run organization.

Two top management committees are of special importance at IBM. The corporate management board at this writing includes the top seventeen executives in the company. The CMB is a concept somewhat akin to a European company's management board, and is not common in the United States.

Generally the CMB is not a decision-making body. Its function is the exchange of information about the company as a whole and open discussion about the business and its prospects. Financial results for the period are presented and discussed. Other matters including the progress of operating units against their plans are reviewed.

The position of the company, its major units and initiatives are presented in full view of the top officers of all the units, whether or not they are directly involved in the matter at hand. One-on-one discussions also occur between the top officers and executives who run divisions and functional units. Decisions are ordinarily taken in the context of the one-on-one meetings. But most significant matters have been or will be disclosed to the entire CMB, so that all top managers in the company are reasonably well appraised of what is occurring everywhere in the company.

For example, financial results—what IBM refers to as the "measurements"—for a group (several divisions) are ordinarily first discussed between the group executive and his or her immediate subordinates who manage the elements of the group. At the group level, measurements for detailed business units are reported by representatives of the corporate financial function to the management team in each group executive's monthly staff meeting. If results are poor, the occasion may result in an open counseling session with other managers present, or in an invitation from the senior executive present to meet privately with those directly involved.

Generally, measurements at the small unit level are also disclosed in the CMB. Because of the earlier discussions, there should be no surprises to those directly involved. But an executive whose area is discussed is sometimes gratified at the attention, sometimes mortified, depending on the results being reported. Further, the company has formal performance appraisals prepared by managers of their subordinates all the way up the chain of command, excluding only the chairman.

Six members of the CMB also serve in a smaller group currently labeled the management committee. The MC includes the senior line and staff officers of the company. The committee generally meets twice a week for half a day each time (unless circumstances require more time). There is a secretariat function for both the CMB and MC which is responsible for the agenda and operations of the CMB and the MC. The committee's secretary estimates that meetings of the committees consume 15 percent of the time of the corporation's top executives.

According to Tom Liptak, vice president of organization and management systems, to which the secretariat function reports, the broad category with which the management committee is concerned includes benefit plans, morale surveys, full employment, and other such issues.

The MC is a decision-making body, though exactly how it comes to its conclusions involves matters of some subtlety. Apparently the MC operates most of the time by consensus. "It is unlikely that with a common understanding of the business," Paul Rizzo, until recently vice chairman of IBM and a member of the management committee, commented to a Harvard Business School class, "we should find ourselves in any basic disagreement."[1]

Despite the importance of the two committees in the management of the corporation, "IBM is not a committee-run company," Tom Liptak points out. The chairman

---

[1] *IBM: The Bubble Memory Incident*, comments by Paul Rizzo to an MBA class at the Harvard Business School, videotaped and copyrighted by Harvard Graduate School of Business Administration, 1979.

has the responsibility for the company's performance, and exercises commensurate authority. The MC does not meet unless the chairman is available. In decision-making, "the chairman's vote is the big one," Liptak says.

The MC and the CMB represent IBM's direct and formal acknowledgment—the committees appear on the organization chart, after all—that several heads function better than one in evaluating issues and coming to a correct conclusion.

The committees also permit the chairman to bring matters of corporate-wide significance to the attention of its high executives in an efficient manner, that is, when they are all assembled to hear.

The significant role which the two committees play in the management of the corporation are not the most unusual aspect of IBM's management system. That honor must go to the unusually influential role of corporate staff.

Staff in a Position of Authority   The top officers of most large companies rely to a degree on staff executives to conduct planning, prepare for contingencies, and see that basic policies of the corporation are carried forward. But in many companies staff executives have a great deal of difficulty in influencing the actions of line managers. This often occurs even in companies in which top management is in agreement with staff executives and tries to support them. The reason is that these companies lack mechanisms by which staff officials can get the attention of top management at the crucial time and in the proper forum. As a result, staff executives often have high-sounding titles and little real influence. Since staff executives often have responsibility for policies which are crucial to the culture of a company, the result of their impotence is that the culture of the organization is weak and key policies are not carried out systematically and comprehensively.

IBM has empowered its staff executives to a

very substantial degree by creating certain procedures which give the staff the opportunity to affect the actions of line organizations, and when they are not heeded, to carry the controversy in a formal and readily accessible way to top management. The ability of corporate staff at IBM to press successfully its views in support of the full employment practice is one of the keys to IBM's successful implementation of employment security for its employees. Two especially important procedures in conveying authority on corporate staff are the contention process and the position of resource manager at the business group or division level.

The Contention Process   At IBM each operating unit prepares plans for periods of varying length—currently an annual, biennial, and five-year plan—detailing the activities to be undertaken and the results expected. Ultimately these plans must be approved by the management committee. But in the process of preparation, draft plans are circulated among the staff functions which review them for consistency with overall corporate objectives. Each staff unit must take a position on the plans of the operating divisions. If staff executives do not agree with the line organization, they must set forth in writing the reasons for their dissent. For example, with respect to full employment, personnel reviews the two- and five-year plans of operating units to make sure that the company has sufficient work for all its employees. Then manufacturing staff studies the adequacy of work-load buffers (subcontracts and other devices, so that if work volume declines, work that has been contracted out can be returned to the company's own plants). Every staff member makes sure that things are being done correctly from their perspective. All is done in an integrated way. If a staff person can't agree with what is being proposed, it is up to him or her to go to the line people to try to resolve the issue.

If upon review of a division's plan or plans, a

staff unit is in agreement with it, the staff unit formally concurs via a written document. Should there be areas of disagreement, the staff function contacts the operating unit and tries to work out the problems. The personnel function, for example, might object that a division's plan shows a head count which is too high, or that the division is overworking its people, or that it lacks sufficient "move tickets," that is, enough money in its budget to relocate people likely to be moved.

Should a disagreement fail to be resolved, the staff unit must either decide to accept the proposal of the business unit or file a formal nonconcurrence. The staff unit cannot be neutral. To fail to file a nonconcurrence is to accept responsibility with the operating unit for the plan. This process is very unusual in American corporations, although not unique. It represents a seriousness of respect for staff contributions to the business. Perhaps it is not surprising that IBM is generally acknowledged to be among the world's best-staffed operations.

What happens to a formal nonconcurrence? Sometimes referred to internally as a "silver bullet," a nonconcurrence is taken very seriously. Upon its filing, a series of meetings between the operating unit and the staff function occur at successively higher levels of the corporation, as resolution of the disagreement is sought. In effect, the contention procedure is a formal method of escalating issues up the chain of command.

The contention process endows staff executives at IBM with real power in the organization. It provides staff with access to top management committees, and thereby with the opportunity to influence the actions of group- and division-level line executives.

The combination of the management committee structure and the contention process combine in IBM to make management of the full-employment practice a reality. The committees permit the chairman to continually reinforce to the top managers in the firm his commitment to the full-employment practice, and to do it in a manner which makes efficient use of his time. The committees also provide a forum to which staff executives responsible for the full-employment practice can report on successes and limitations of the effort. Without the committee structure communications would be far more difficult.

The contention process permits staff executives to raise issues with operating groups which are acting in ways inconsistent with full employment. Such actions, or plans, could include too rapid hiring, failure to have contingency plans for a downturn, refusal to hire persons displaced elsewhere in IBM, and failure to budget sufficient resources for retraining and remissioning. Through the contention process, disagreements about such matters can be escalated up the management chain, giving the staff executives both exposure and influence.

How the executive committee structure and the contention process contributed to the management of full employment during IBM's business downturn in 1985–87 will be our topic after first examining how IBM prepares to meet its full employment obligation.

Hiring: The Last Desperate Act of a Full Employment Company   Employment security is very important. It is a key to the commitment of IBMers to the company, and is a major factor in the company's outstanding long-term performance.

IBM is successful as a full-employment company because of its ability to balance its resources. This section tells how IBM implements full employment by making resource balancing a way of life.

Resource balancing includes techniques such as minimizing hiring and buffering the work force. These are cautionary practices which position the company to continue to provide work for its employees if and when a business downturn occurs.

"When you, as a manager," begins an article in IBM's internal management journal, "hire a regular, full-time employee, you are making a multimillion-dollar decision for IBM. Over the course of an employee's 25- or 30-year career, the company can invest millions in salary, benefits and education."[2] To avoid hiring wherever possible, the company urges its managers to eliminate, postpone, or reprioritize work and also to increase the efficiency of current operations. When these avenues are exhausted, managers are told to look to existing employees who are available and can be redeployed and/or retrained. Sometime temporary assignments or overtime are possible. Finally, work may be contracted out or done by supplemental or contract (i.e., short term) employees. Work subcontracted or performed by nonregular employees is referred to as a buffer.

The use of subcontracts and supplemental or contract employees in order to preserve future work opportunities for regular employees is a matter of controversy. It is sometimes commented that full-employment companies do not really deserve the name because they use temporary workers or contract out work. The presumption is apparently that a full-employment company should provide employment security for everyone associated with it. This view ignores several realities, however, and should therefore be rejected. Specialization may permit companies which are subcontractors to offset declines in work from IBM by work from other customers, so that declines in IBM's work load are not necessarily felt by its subcontractors. Also, college students, retirees, and employees on leaves of absence from other firms

---

[2] "To Hire or Not to Hire: Balancing the Alternatives," *IBM Management Report*, May 1987, p. 12.

may want temporary or part-time jobs. Nonetheless, the use of buffers does tend to shift unemployment from IBM regular employees to nonregular employees when IBM's business declines.

IBM buffers its work force in order to provide full employment for its regular employees, and thereby gain certain advantages (which are spelled out in the next chapter). From the company's perspective this is sufficient reason for using a buffer. But from a broader social perspective, it may have some disadvantages. This would be the case particularly if some people were encouraged to stay in the buffer and absorb a disproportionate amount of the burden of business downturns.

IBM maintains that it attempts to minimize hardships placed on nonregular employees. Nonregulars know the terms and conditions of their employment up front. Ordinarily, employment is for a period not to exceed six months, though in some instances, as in 1987–88, the period is extended to one year.

Generally, nonregulars complete their term of employment, so that the company does not simply dump these employees unexpectedly when business declines. The company staggers its hiring so that reductions in force can be spread out over time while permitting nonregulars to serve their full term.

An important element of resource balancing and cost control at IBM involves the use of vacation time. Ordinarily the company's employees use about 87 percent of their vacation and place in a vacation "bank" the remaining 13 percent. When a downturn in the business occurs, the company asks employees to take accrued vacations, thereby reducing excess employment and cutting costs (since banked vacation is an additional cost item to the company in an accounting sense).

In 1986, company executives debated whether

or not to require employees to take banked vacation allotment and the year's full vacation allotment. The decision was to approach the matter voluntarily. "There was no reason to believe the employees wouldn't do what the company needed," George Krawiec observed, "so we decided, 'Let's ask them.' "

Informed about the company's business situation and the need to have vacation used, employees in 1986 took 107 percent of the vacation allowable that year (drawing down vacation banks for the time beyond 100 percent).

In the area of vacation, all IBMers were touched by the company's business downturn, not simply those who were redeployed.

In many IBM units at the group and division level there are resource managers whose responsibilities include assisting senior management in the maintenance of full employment. In order to try to balance work load against staff numbers in the long term, these managers try to minimize hiring and use overtime, transfers, and other devices. Harry Bernhard is a retired IBM executive who now teaches at the University of Southern California and whose responsibilities at various times in his career involved resource balancing. From the point of view of the resource manager, every new hire is a potential problem of placement in a business downturn. Hence, resource managers try to persuade line managers to minimize hiring. This is never easy in a corporation as accustomed to growth as IBM. Yet only when no other avenue of getting necessary work done remains will a resource manager be comfortable with hiring.

"The last desperate act of a full-employment company," said Harry Bernhard, "is to make a full-time hire."

Because the corporate commitment under full employment to each new hire is so substantial, managers are urged to look for candidates who have the flexibility and potential to change with the company, not simply the ability to handle an immediate task.

At IBM every manager is charged with a basic responsibility to hire the best-qualified person available to fill a position. The company emphasizes to its managers the importance of "total assessment" in making hiring decisions—that is, of evaluating the total person using all appropriate sources of information available. In some cases there are objective tests that have been validated for use in specific job categories. The company independently verifies information provided by applicants regarding education, employment experience, and criminal records, if any. Beyond such objective measures, hiring managers are encouraged to utilize an accomplishment-based selection rationale to assess what the applicant has accomplished academically, in prior work experience, in areas of extracurricular or community leadership, or other personal accomplishments that can be demonstrative of high levels of ability, drive, motivation, leadership, and work ethic. The only absolutely hard standards the company applies to hiring, that is, those other than the informed judgment of its managers, are that it refuses to hire those who have lied on their applications or show evidence of use of nonmedically prescribed controlled substances.

"I looked for character when hiring," said Dick Jacquemard, a retired IBM manufacturing executive whom we met at Boulder. "I asked myself, 'Is this the kind of person I want to hire? Is that person qualified to do the job?' I think 80 percent of the people I hired could be retrained in any type of manufacturing job. People can relearn skills. Nobody is not retrainable. At IBM that philosophy has helped us hire people for life."

But other IBM managers say they hire only for the job at hand. The discrepancy is accounted for in part by the role of the personnel office, which does the preliminary screening of applicants for skills and accomplishments.

Because they have been so carefully selected, current IBM employees are often preferred over new hires by managers who have vacancies to fill. "I prefer not to hire from the outside," said Sandy August. "An IBMer may not know the job well, but he or she knows the company." This attitude, which appears to be widespread among IBM managers, helps explain the company's ability to fill the great majority of its positions by promotion from within.

Individuality and Teamwork   Many managers struggle with the apparent contradiction between dealing with employees as individuals and encouraging them to work together in teams. They fear that if a team effort is broken into individual contributions, and team members are rewarded differently for their differing contributions, the team's cohesion will be broken up. Unable to mix individuality and teamwork, they opt for one or the other. In the Western world managers have tended in recent years to favor individual treatment over teamwork. In the Far East managers have favored team effort over individuality. These differences in managerial approach are often ascribed to basic cultural differences between the West and the East.

One of the most impressive things about IBM's management system is that it combines both individuality and teamwork. The company has developed the ability to harness for business purposes both elements of the human personality: the desire for individual recognition and the wish to be part of a group. By so doing, it achieves much of the best of the different cultural traditions of East and West. Combining the two traditions, the company is often able to achieve very high levels of human performance that exceed what can be attained by relying on either individualism or group cohesion alone.

How is this difficult combination achieved?

Let us look first at individuality. At IBM every

employee's performance is evaluated annually by his or her immediate manager. Salary increases and promotion opportunities are determined by the performance rating of the individual. All IBM employees are salaried, and the performance appraisal system extends from manufacturing workers through the members of the corporation's management committee, who are each evaluated by the company's chairman. Identifying and rewarding individual contribution is one of the most important aspects of IBM's corporate culture.

Simultaneously, the company is continually placing its employees in teams, task forces, project units, and similar groups in which they cooperate to accomplish business objectives. The success of individuals in these group activities are evaluated by their managers as part of the individual's performance appraisal process. The combination of individual assessment and team involvement seems to work. IBMers who leave the company are often struck by the lesser degree of cooperation among employees at other companies.

Joe Taylor retired from IBM when the Greencastle facility was closed and went to work for a private university. He contrasted IBM with his new company and in the process tried to express the apparent paradox by which IBM is able both to treat people as individuals and to have them cooperate in teams.

"In IBM we try to treat people as individuals. I see some of that in my new employer, but much more can be done. And I don't see the teamwork we had at IBM. At IBM, if you had a problem, you could go to anybody and they'd help you. That was the fun part of working at IBM. They'd even loan a manager some people if he had to get the work out fast.

"When I hired people at IBM," Joe continued, "I always asked, 'Are you a team player? Do you work well in teams?' I could tell by a person's reaction if he or she was willing to jump in and help."

To reinforce teamwork the company continually stresses to its employees how special a place IBM is to work. It trains its managers on an ongoing basis how to get people to work together and in the best methods of small-group management. And it enforces, primarily by peer pressure, behavior codes that extend even to dress.

"There's a view in the outside world," said Gerry Marmion, a manager at the San Jose facility, "that we as IBMers all go marching to the same drummer. Nothing could be further from the truth. People should not confuse our clothes with intellectual conformity."

Challenged about why IBMers generally appear in business suits (usually blue), white shirts, and ties, he insisted that "not all IBMers dress like this. Those who do dress this way usually have to meet with customers and the general public, where we don't want our appearance to detract from the more important business at hand."

He continued with a story. An IBM executive was invited to give a speech to a local business group. Knowing the stereotyped view that exists, he began his speech by telling everyone in the audience, most of whom were casually attired, that he felt he had a good idea of what they expected and didn't want to disappoint them. He pointed out to them his three-piece pinstripe suit, his wingtip shoes, and his "sincere" tie. "You know," he said, turning to the audience, "it's hell renting this stuff!"

Today's business dress at IBM stresses the yellow tie, a style apparently established, probably unknowingly, by John Akers in a photograph which appeared on the cover of a national magazine. When the magazine appeared, many IBM executives suddenly appeared in yellow ties similar to the one Akers wore. Rumor in the corporation has it that the tinier the dots on the yellow tie, the greater its power.

Still, IBMers insist that outsiders should not read too much conformity into the similarity in dress. "Because we dress alike doesn't mean we think alike," Gerry insists. And he is right. The company is also known for significant internal disagreements, which the contention system, operating in various forms through all levels of the corporation, is designed to resolve.

IBM managers are dress-conscious and status-conscious. Yet offices are largely unadorned, all of basically the same size, and are not treated as the property of their occupants. When an IBM executive is traveling, his or her office is ordinarily available for use by other IBM executives who are visiting. Managers, like other employees, are willing to help each other out and do whatever is necessary to make the business go. When the San Jose plant early in 1987 asked for volunteers to go onto the production floor to help relieve a critical backlog in production, several managers from other functions were among those who volunteered.

At IBM such group-like behavior as unofficial dress codes, effective teamwork, and people willing to forgo perks and status to get work done are combined with individual recognition and reward. Conformity in some areas does not prevent disagreements and controversies about what is the best course for the company. The combination of teamwork and individuality encourages people to help out in crises and assures them that they will be recognized for their contribution. Hence it is a key element in IBM's ability to cope with a rising and falling business load without having to sacrifice its full-employment objective.

HOW TO MANAGE FOR FULL EMPLOYMENT:

Part 2. Making Things Happen

Chapter Eight

Getting the Functions to Work Together   All organizations experience rivalries and antagonisms among different units. In business it is common for manufacturing and marketing to have tensions; for staff and line units to be jealous of one another; for headquarters and field personnel to be disrespectful each of the other. In many companies these tensions pose almost insurmountable barriers to effective cooperation across organizational lines. Where such barriers exist, a company is seriously handicapped in executing broad programs.

Exhortations and pleas to cooperate by top executives to managers in a company's various units may do some good, but they are not enough. Recognizing this, IBM has created procedures and committees to make a reality of the teamwork dream of different functions working together.

When business downturns occur, IBM's careful selection of people permits it to make adjustments that would be difficult for other companies, and its management systems allow it to manage the adjustment process. In the company, when executives speak of "resource," as they often do, they generally are referring to the corporation's employees. Reflecting this emphasis, the corporation has over many decades created a sequence of committees whose responsibility has been to make efficient allocations of the company's people. During the 1985–87 recession, the company utilized a number of already existing committees to balance and allocate human resources so as to avoid the necessity to lay off people.

Group Resource Directors (the GRD)   Certain committees concerned with resource balancing in the corporation were already in existence when softness appeared in the business in 1985. In particular, the corporate resource group (CRG) had been established in December 1974, consisting of the corporate functional staff heads, from, specifically, marketing, service, manufacturing, management information systems/

administration, finance, and personnel. The function of the CRG was to protect full employment, manage any major imbalances which developed, and control the growth in the corporation's employee population in order to control costs.

In 1983 the resource management committee had been established. It consisted of the assistant business group executives, the corporation's vice president of personnel, and the IBM director of budgets. This committee met monthly and was responsible for the following:

■ the overall direction of resource management in the U.S.
■ financial considerations
■ full employment protections and rebalancing activities (including, for example, remissioning and redeployment)
■ giving or refusing hiring approval to operating units on a quarterly basis

The personnel function at IBM is responsible for establishing the framework in which resource balancing actions such as redeployment proceed, but line or general managers carried out the individual actions. General managers were being trained for their role in full employment throughout their IBM careers. Each IBM manager is expected to receive forty hours per year of managerial training, 60 percent of which is in the corporation's people-management policies and practices.

As part of its responsibility, the corporate personnel staff, headed by George Krawiec, corporate-level manager of resource assessment and planning, updated situation-specific plans for how to balance resources in any eventuality, from a business downturn to a total collapse. These plans became a framework upon which the detailed resource balancing of the 1985–87 downturn was based.

When in 1985 the business slowdown became apparent, the corporation shifted its full-employment activities from general oversight to active involvement. The resource management committee was replaced by a committee of the business group resource directors, and representatives of corporate personnel and finance. Labeled the group resource directors (GRD), the committee met twice a month. Its objective was to protect full employment in the downturn. To do this it had several functions:

■ to identify in which major skills and in which units there were surpluses and whatever needs for those skills existed elsewhere in the company.

■ to develop solutions which would alleviate the developing surpluses such as redeployment, retraining, or work movement (i.e., moving work to people rather than people to work).

■ to avoid additional hiring in the company by developing alternatives, wherever possible.

■ to utilize other cost-savings solutions as available, including reduced use of subcontractors, supplemental employees, and overtime, and to ask employees to take earned and deferred vacation in order to cut costs.

During the years of the business downturn, this committee became the key agency by which IBM managed its remissioning, redeployment, and other efforts to preserve full employment. The composition of the committee was carefully chosen, and was not representative of the company as a whole. Instead, the elements of the company which were to be most involved in the actual rebalancing of the corporation's facilities and people were chosen to be on the committee. In 1985–87 these elements were manufacturing, programming, and administration.

Senders and Receivers   In essence the GRD had three elements represented: those units which were sending people out as they downsized, especially manufacturing and development, but also business group and corporate administrative staff; those units which were receiving people, especially the marketing or sales functions; and personnel and finance, which

served as referees of a sort for the transactions between senders and receivers. Meeting frequently, the GRD worked out
the transference of thousands of employees among functions
and locations, attempting to match the needs of the receiving
units to the skills and capabilities of people from the sending
units. Retraining programs were also identified. Line management made every selection. The individual employee voluntarily accepted the job offer. In effect, representatives from
the corporate staff brought willing senders and receivers
together.

"Line management did an excellent job getting
people interested in redeployment," said Ken Ranftle, a personnel executive. "We didn't have to push people. They volunteered. If you make it clear to people that we want to build
up relations with our customers and it will enhance their
careers to be in the field, then many volunteer readily. Our
work force wants to be where the action is."

The personnel function at sending and receiv-
ing sites, acting in concert with the GRD and working through
line management, contacted candidates, obtained space for
interviews, sponsored seminars on what it is like to live in
this or that community, and generally facilitated the redeployment process.

Charles Hawkins, the personnel director representing the marketing group on the GRD, described how
incentives were used to get field sales offices to hire redeployed
employees. "On the receiver side, we had to have groups
willing to take people. We enticed the field by saying that
there would be no penalty if they took redeployed employees
[i.e., the funding for the new people was added to the existing
field staffing budget]. Once we removed the financial handi-
caps, the field could accept qualified candidates. This allowed
the field to increase marketing staff with experienced IBM
people."

When there are resource surpluses in the business, hiring is restricted in the areas which need additional resources. This control ensures that managers who need additional people will find them internally and thereby solve the company's surplus problem.

In addition, the company attempts to provide a climate in which its managers are generally receptive to a redeployment initiative and see some advantage in participating in it. As part of the training that managers receive, the importance of the full-employment practice is stressed so that managers will be willing to participate in redeployment. Managers know that they may be a redeployment sender or receiver at different points in time and appreciate how this can work for them in either case.

The GRD did much of the basic work involved in remissioning and redeployment. It helped prepare guidelines for local managers in how to do redeployment which were the framework upon which site-level resource managers, such as those at Boulder and Greencastle, placed site-specific approaches. In the specific instance of Boulder, for example, guidelines were prepared by several managers from Boulder and corporate and division staff people because of their familiarity with the redeployment effort. A mini-GRD process was established at Boulder, including people from each function. The committee also established transfer-out and transfer-in teams to assist the individuals involved in those two processes.

In Boulder, managers received the guidelines book, and a site resource balancing office was set up. In addition, there were transfer teams for each of the product lines.

Group resource managers were themselves experienced in placing excess employees within IBM. The best of them, as described by Harry Bernhard, knew the market within IBM for people with the kind of skills his or her units possessed. "If I was five hundred people over," Harry said of his own period as a resource manager, "I knew who'd left us in the past—what kind of skills they possessed—and I knew what divisions had taken my people. I knew my human in-ventory and what its propensity was." Bernhard had to know both what divisions would be likely to hire his people and where his people might like to go, because each individual always had to decide for himself or herself whether or not to take the positions offered from within the company. Each resource director took pride in placing people as much as possible without their feeling any pressure to accept an offer.

"In my division," Harry Bernhard said, "if an employee were being reassigned due to reorganization and was resisting, I would kick it up the chain of command one level each day, so that a final result would be achieved in three days. It was the role of personnel, as I saw it, to be sure that draconian measures were not taken."

A final check to see that draconian measures are not taken involves IBM's open door policy by which any employee can take a question or issue to the corporation's chairman, John Akers. For each open door concern Akers receives a full report and summary, an investigator's report, and a draft letter to the employee. No IBM executive wants to have his or her poor treatment of an employee who is being relocated or redeployed become the occasion of an open door complaint to Mr. Akers.

What makes the various elements of the cor-poration work together to make the redeployment process successful? In summary, the company has
- units wanting to send people and units wanting to receive them;
- the commitment and oversight of top-level management;
- incentives to line managers to make it work;
- a culture to translate the process into something positive for people to do to advance their careers; and

■ checks and balances (such as the speak out program or the open door) to see that individuals are treated fairly.

Getting People Prepared Via a Communications Program   A corporate initiative is much more likely to be effectively implemented in the field if the organization's people, at all levels and in all locations, understand what it is, why it is being undertaken, and what their own role is likely to be. Many companies understand this, and send communications to their employees. But frequently the communication efforts fail, either because managers and employees do not pay attention to the messages, or because the messages themselves are so ill-timed and poorly prepared that they are ineffectual.

In both timing and content IBM's communication efforts during the 1985–87 downturn were effective. The corporation's communication program about redeployment and remissioning was begun a bit prior to the efforts themselves. Ursula Fairbairn and Walt Burdick realized that the best way for employees to understand what the company was doing was through an effective communication plan, and they worked with the corporate communications staff on a specific program which would be implemented throughout the redeployment period.

Articles in IBM's corporate journal *Think* explained the redeployment effort broadly. At Boulder and Greencastle a person from the communications staff was on the task forces for the remissioning and the closing from the start. Communication with employees was never an afterthought, but a crucial piece of each site's action plan from its inception. It was the responsibility of the site managers at Boulder, Greencastle, and Westlake to communicate the decisions about each site and the options of employees, but the corporation assisted them, and simultaneously reminded them of their communications obligation by sending them checklists and advice about what to do. Guidelines read, for example: "Get the information to employees *fast*. Don't tell them on a Friday."

But there was more to it than this. As explained by Les Simon, IBM director of employee and management communications, the communications programs themselves were intended to accomplish a specific objective. This is one of the things which made the IBM communication plan outstanding. Information was not being given to employees simply for their enlightenment. It was not merely background knowledge that was being provided. Instead, the literature, videotapes, and bulletin board notices were intended to send employees to their direct managers for assistance and were to alert the managers that employees would be coming to them. The managers in their turn were being prepared by the company to handle employee inquiries by literature and training programs provided specifically to management. A couple of days before the company makes a major announcement and conveys it to its employees, a question-and-answer package is sent to all managers so that they are prepared to answer employees' inquiries.

The following paragraphs are an excerpt from a question-and-answer package prepared for managers to assist them in discussing a redeployment initiative with employees:

Q: How long do I have to decide if I am going to accept or reject a job offer?

A: Employees are encouraged to make a decision as soon as possible so management can plan accordingly and permit the employee sufficient time to properly consider relocations. Generally, a decision should be made within five to ten days of receiving the offer.

Q: *What considerations will be given if both husband and wife are employed by IBM and only one is associated with the work that is being transferred?*

A: An IBM-employed spouse of a relocated IBM employee will be eligible for the following assistance:
■ priority placement consideration for up to one year
■ personal leave of absence for up to one year
■ priority consideration for supplemental employment while on leave
■ retraining internally for an IBM job
■ reimbursement of some outside employment/counseling services

Q: *How do you expect to accomplish this redeployment?*

A: Our plan is to accomplish this on a voluntary basis.

Q: *Will employees get salary increases upon transferring?*

A: At the time of reassignment, each individual's salary will be reviewed. If appropriate, salary increases will be granted in accordance with IBM's merit pay philosophy and current compensation guidelines.

Complex questions may be referred by managers to staff specialists, of course.

In announcing the initial redeployment efforts, the company informed its employees that the field sales staff would be expanded. Simultaneously, employees were told that manufacturing and headquarters staffs would be pared. As has been described in earlier chapters, many IBMers saw the opportunity to change careers by going into field marketing, and went to their direct managers to volunteer for a change in assignment.

Similarly, when the corporation announced an

early retirement incentive in the fall of 1986, employees read about the program in the corporation's literature and went to their managers to apply.

IBM's philosophy is to rely on the tie between direct manager and employee and to reinforce it continually. Since the company wants its managers to handle matters involving employees, corporate communications are used to encourage employees to talk to their managers. Managers read the corporate communications to learn what employees will be asking them about.

Also, by including managers in such a direct and significant way in the communications process, the company compels its managers to be aware of corporate policies and to be responsible for them. The very common cop-out used by supervisors in many companies of denying responsibility for corporate policies—"I'd like to help you, George, you know I'm your friend, but those sons-of-guns in corporate made it this way; you'll have to go deal with them"—is difficult to do in IBM.

Finally, one of the reasons IBM is successful with its communications programs is that it has built up a reservoir of goodwill among employees and in the communities in which it operates. Communications and public relations do not substitute for goodwill, but where good feelings exist, communications can do its job much better. IBM devotes considerable effort and resources to preserving the reservoir of goodwill, as we have seen in the chapters above.

Line Management Buy-in   One of the most difficult challenges in any organization is to get line managers to take time from their busy schedules to implement corporate programs. It is generally all too easy for them to listen politely to a corporate initiative which has the long-run interests of the organization at heart and then never get around to doing much about the program.

This is a natural human response, but one which is very destructive in an organization. To counter it, IBM uses two primary methods. One is frequent training and development activities. IBM provides formal training at each level of management, as well as regular updates during a manager's career. A new manager receives a week of formal training at the corporate level and an additional thirty days orientation at the division level. Thereafter, the company's target is for every manager to receive forty hours of annual training, which includes thirty-two hours of people management. The emphasis in training is on fundamentals, by which IBM means interpersonal skills, personnel policies and practices, communications, basic management techniques, and beliefs and culture. Supporting these content areas is a basic mission for management development activities which includes the following objectives:

- to pass on the company's heritage.
- to strengthen the manager-employee relationship.
- to reinforce and build managerial skills.
- to keep managers well-informed about internal and external developments impacting the business.

Training content is continually updated through a needs analysis which relies on employee opinion surveys, a review of management activities, and utilizes an advisory council for recommendations about keeping current. Through its management training activities, the company keeps managers knowledgeable about what needs to be done in the company and involved in the effort to get things accomplished.

A second method of engaging managers in the corporation's initiatives is to demonstrate top management attention to corporate programs via review meetings, so that subordinate managers know that their performance on corporate programs is reported to the top and is an important aspect of their overall performance.

In the 1985–87 effort, most redeploys were first apprised by their immediate managers of the job opportunity they eventually took. This fact speaks well for IBM managers. Ordinarily, supervisors are reluctant to part with good employees, since the performance of their units may be adversely affected. Yet IBM managers searched out eager and ambitious people who could successfully handle new careers and pointed them away from their existing jobs.

Asked why they did so, managers gave various answers. Some said that the company needed the people elsewhere and so they felt they should release those who wanted to go. Others said that their units were going to be reduced anyway, so that there was no ability to hoard people regardless. Finally, others noted that the reception and surrender of people was a common cycle in the company, "the way the game is played," and that they relinquished good people in the expectation that at some later date they would receive good people into their own units. Because there is so much movement of managers in IBM, managers were satisfied to have good people well distributed in the company, presuming that as they moved they would encounter organizations staffed by good people.

Retraining and redeployment are a way of life in IBM, so that a certain amount goes on continually. But the effort in 1985–87 was on a much larger scale than usual. Because of this, the corporate management board wanted to follow closely the redeployment and remissioning efforts. Ursula Fairbairn (and later Sherry Lambly) was the personnel executive who co-chaired the GRD with a line executive during its most active period. Once a month they reported personally to the CMB in such detail that even the resolution of specific site situations was described. "It was our task to be sure that none of us lost sight of the people involved," she said. "Our reporting to the CMB was continuing evidence that the top officers of the corporation cared about what was happening to the people and that not one person would get lost in the size of the company and the complexity of the process."

Measuring and Monitoring   IBM believes that no significant business effort can be accounted a success unless it or aspects of it can somehow be made measurable and monitored. This is especially true in a large organization in which efforts are certain to get lost in the urgency of day-to-day operations unless they are separately identified and accounted for. In its redeployment and remissioning effort, IBM established measurements and monitored them continually.

The redeployment process was complex. Sherry Lambly's report to the CMB at the end of May 1987 showed some 7,100 people to have been redeployed since 1985. Of these, marketing and sales had received the majority.

The report also showed many persons transferred from the headquarters staffs to the field marketing and sales staffs. By May 1987, Sherry told the CMB some 2,177 headquarters people had accepted assignments to the field.

But this was just the tip of the iceberg. For each person who was redeployed, there were several people who shifted jobs. This was because in some instances it was necessary to move two or three people in manufacturing in order to free a single person who was qualified by aptitude and interest to go into sales. In order to have a net transfer of 7,100, many more job moves were required.

Sherry also reported to the CMB on the transfer of work into facilities which were being remissioned in whole or in part. Work involving some 2,627 positions had been transferred among facilities in order to provide work to otherwise redundant people without requiring them to relocate. These were primarily transfers of work into facilities in which manufacturing had excess personnel. Boulder, for ex-

ample, had received a net infusion of work for 648 individuals
by the end of May 1987.

By the next monthly report of the GRD these
numbers had all become obsolete, as the efforts of the corporation to remission and redeploy continued. Finally, the
May report of the GRD to the top managers of the corporation described the status of the closing of the IBM facilities
in Greencastle, Indiana, and Westlake, California.

Behind each presentation to the CMB lay an
extensive managerial effort in which the contention process
played an important role. As each operating unit of IBM
prepared its annual business plan for submission to the management committee for review and ultimate approval, George
Krawiec, Sherry Lambly, and their colleagues reviewed the
proposed plans for their consistency with the company's resource balancing objectives. When plans were presented by
the units' top managers to the MC, the managers making the
presentation were required to state verbally whether or not
there were any nonconcurrences. If there were, the objections
were heard verbally, just as the plans received verbal presentation, and handled by the chairman or the MC as a team.
Because of their ability to raise nonconcurrences, the resource
balancing staff had considerable influence in affecting the
plans of the business groups and operating divisions.

After the presentation of the individual units'
plans to the MC, the planning staff rolled them up (i.e., compiled them) into a comprehensive document and reviewed the
whole for its internal consistency and practicality. Once
again, the resource balancing staff participated in this review.
At its conclusion the MC gave by letter specific approval to
each business unit to execute its plan.

With the plans in operation, the finance staff
received monthly reports on the measures and relayed them
to the CMB at its meetings. The measurement reports identified the units' goals and the variance of actual performance

from them. Corporate staff could call top management's attention to the failure or success—whether the unit involved was a sender or receiver of surplus personnel.

During the 1985–87 rebalancing, direct involvement with the management committee and the corporate management board was of special importance to the resource balancing staff. Thousands of IBMers were crossing major lines in the organization—from manufacturing to sales, from headquarters to the field. These transfers could sometimes be dealt with only at the top of the company, since the units involved reported to the same boss only at that level.

Why was the resource balancing staff given such frequent access to the top management of the corporation to report about its progress? I asked this question of Sherry Lambly.

"Because the chairman, John Akers, asked to see it," she replied.

In the end, what made the corporation's substantial remissioning and redeployment effort succeed was a combination of top-management support on a continuing basis, effective staff work by the resource balancing team, and the willingness and participation of line management. The management committee, the corporate management board, and the group resource directors were the administrative mechanisms by which the necessary communications, planning, and review were accomplished.

The Outcome: How People Felt About the Redeployment Effort   A project or a program is not over when it is completed. There remains a process of review so that elements of success or failure can be assessed and lessons learned. At IBM, not the least of the learning involved how the people involved felt about the program in which they had participated. IBM interviewed its employees via attitude surveys and debriefed its managers about the effort.

Generally, people felt good about their involvement in the redeployment effort in its immediate aftermath. For many people who had undertaken new careers, years will have to pass before a final verdict can be reached, however. But for staff and line executives involved in managing the program, it was a good experience.

By leaving employees and managers with a generally good opinion of the redeployment and remissioning efforts, IBM had created the opportunity to do the same again, should the occasion arise.

By mid-1987 the business crisis was lessening. Indications of higher sales were emerging. The GRD no longer met every two weeks, but now only once a month. The full cycle of a major rebalancing was being completed.

Remissioning and Redeployment in Europe   How far can a multinational company go in promulgating uniform corporate policies in different lands? Can full employment be made a reality in the maze of national cultures and differing legal requirements?

It is remarkable the degree to which IBM has been able to create a measure of uniformity in its business personality throughout the world. In Europe, for example, John Stanley, directeur général des operations for IBM Europe, commented that it is difficult to explain how IBM is able to do this. "There is no European culture," he said. "We can't come to an agreement among the twelve EEC countries. What we try to do in IBM Europe is to manage the differences while establishing our own corporate fundamentals alongside the country culture."

Yet the company's three basic values seem to

be at such a basic level that people of very different cultures have little or no difficulty in buying into them.

The European Maze   Despite IBM's success in maintaining full employment in Europe, redeployment and remissioning can be more complicated to execute than in the United States. In Germany, for example, the company must obtain the consent of the government-created works councils for the redeployment of *each person*. In France, the company must advise the works councils of its plans and receive their advice, but the works councils cannot oppose management's decision if the company has followed the proper procedures in dealing with the councils.

The national orientation of governments and the cultural differences of people combine to make providing full employment difficult. This is ironic because European nations have many legal requirements intended to make layoffs difficult in order to help preserve people's jobs.

European legal requirements concerning management-labor relations vary from systems much like that in the United States, which are found in the United Kingdom and Denmark; the codetermination of Scandinavia, the Netherlands, and Germany; the highly politicized conflict of France, Italy, and Spain; the company-focused unionism of Greece, Turkey, and Finland; and the voluntary processes of Switzerland and Belgium. In France, Italy and Spain, the processes followed in labor-management relations are the primary concern of the law. In Germany, the Netherlands, and Sweden, the substance of what results is of greater concern.

To move employees across national borders sometimes requires visas. The European tradition of craft unions makes more difficult the transfer of people out of their functional training. The company needs to create an environment in which a person can move with dignity to a second or third career, John Stanley remarked, something that seems alien to the thinking of many Europeans.

In general, the maze of national jurisdictions and complex legal requirements slow down processes of adjustment by corporations to changes in the business situation. Where consultation with works councils is required, it takes longer to launch programs. Where there is delay, there are also greater costs and the risks of being too late.

Despite the great differences in setting, IBM's subsidiaries throughout the world (South America to Japan) struggle to find a way within each national system to make full employment a reality.

There is one great advantage to a full-employment company that is missing in the United States. By law in many European nations, a layoff must be accompanied by a social plan which the company prepares and which details the benefits laid-off employees and affected communities will receive. These plans can be expensive and time-consuming both to prepare and implement. By providing full employment and moving work to people, IBM largely avoids these costs.

IBM Europe entered at a somewhat later date the business downturn which first afflicted the American company in 1985. Officially, IBM Europe, with its headquarters in Paris, began to encourage major redeployment and remissioning steps by its national subsidiaries in the fall of 1986. IBM Germany, however, catching sight of the coming downturn earlier than most, had initiated some actions to limit hiring and redeploy people as early as December 1985.

Adjustment in Europe took much the form that it had in the United States. Headquarters staff was scheduled for a 35 percent reduction over two years. Sending functions are personnel, communications, and general services. Receiving functions are finance, business planning, and marketing. In several countries manufacturing employment was reduced and field sales personnel increased.

The executive committee of IBM Europe is the top decision-making body and is somewhat similar to the management committee at corporate headquarters in the United States. The committee meets every Monday and Friday to review operations and propositions set forth by the staff.

Each country has a resource balancer head who works closely with a manufacturing executive, a personnel executive, and a marketing executive, who together constitute the country resource management committee. In IBM Europe, the program is currently managed and monitored by Jacques Auboin, group director of resource management. Auboin meets every month with the country resource balancer executive to assess results. In these countries, the resource management committee meets monthly with the executive committee as well.

To manage the redeployment effort, the country resource management executive established the following guidelines for the countries:

■ set redeployment targets for functional top executives.

■ establish committees of experienced managers, so-called pro shops, to manage the process effectively.

■ establish a communications program to support the redeployment effort by causing employees interested in new careers to go to their managers for referral; the communications program included bulletin-board announcements, a letter to employees from the general manager of each subsidiary, a meeting to train managers, a package of materials for managers about redeployment, visitations to sending facilities by receiving groups, and visitations by employees interested in redeployment to the sites of possible new jobs for them.

■ identification of employee "surplus" and "openings" by site, functions, and skills.

■ identification of retraining needs and educational curricula.

■ identification on a monthly basis of the movement of work to areas of employee surplus, and

■ monthly reports as to the quantitative status of the redeployment and remissioning effort.

By the end of September 1987, one year after the start of the redeployment effort in Europe, more than three thousand people had been transferred into field marketing, and the resource management executive was keeping a record country by country of people transferring into field sales and from other functions. Yet, as in the United States, the three thousand net transfers were only the tip of the iceberg. To achieve the net transfers, twice that many additional job moves had to be made.

Remissioning **A**msterdam   In some instances it is not possible to find work within a nation's borders for all the employees who need to be redeployed. When that happens, work must be moved to the people, and if that involves movement from one nation to another, the process can be sensitive.

At Amsterdam, IBM had a plant producing ball-head typewriters and printers and employing some fifteen hundred manufacturing personnel. As business softened, it became too costly to continue to manufacture in Amsterdam. There were not sufficient other missions within Holland which could be moved to Amsterdam to provide enough employment to present people being redeployed out of production. Some people retired early, and others accepted redeployment to field marketing, but still there were excess employees at Amsterdam. The resource committe in IBM Europe began to search for what they termed a "credible backfill"—that is, a mission which could be moved into Amsterdam for good business reasons.

The transformation of Amsterdam created the opportunity to relocate the core of IBM's parts distribution operation in Paris. The Netherlands was believed to be a more efficient location from which to get parts from point to point within a twenty-four-hour period than the then location in France. Discussions toward this end were begun by IBM France with the works council of the facility and the works council of IBM France. When employment was found for the French employees affected, and the basis of the corporation's decision was explained, the French councils took a formal position of neutrality on the matter, and the transfer of work to Amsterdam was made. IBM Europe attempted to keep the intended transfer of work into Amsterdam secret until the discussions in France were completed, but rumors leaked out in the Netherlands, causing a certain embarrassment in France. Nonetheless, a sensitive issue of work-balancing in a multinational context had been successively resolved.

When the transfer took place, the company had forty to fifty trucks per day moving equipment from Paris to Amsterdam for almost two months. The backbone of parts logistics in Europe was moved from France to the Netherlands, but employees were not moved.

This was a very different result than when the Westlake facility was moved to Boulder, Colorado, in the United States. There, many employees made the transfer from California to Colorado, although distance was greater and the climate far more different than from Paris to the Netherlands.

Summary of Lessons Learned

■ A company can build the capacity to execute its policies and practices effectively. This is fully as important as developing a business strategy, and is often much more difficult.
■ Careful management can develop both a capacity for teamwork in an organization and a practice of identifying and rewarding individual contributions. The combination of the two permits human performance to be maximized.

■ The secret to effective execution is to have lower-level managers and employees committed to corporate goals, and this is accomplished by having each person who has a role feel that he or she is the one doing the most significant things.

■ The recipe to achieve this kind of individual commitment is complex and includes some surprising ingredients. Specifically, a company must

—provide continuing evidence of top management commitment and oversight.

—build a culture via training and top-executive attention that includes an employee-comes-first attitude.

—delegate to middle managers discretion in how to carry out the mission assigned to them so long as actions taken are consistent with the corporate philosophy.

—place key corporate staff executives who are responsible for the policies and practices in positions of authority and influence with respect to line managers.

—provide staff executives as catalysts whose job it is to get different line organizations and staff units to work together (e.g., manufacturing and marketing, headquarters and field personnel, etc.).

—develop extensive and timely communications to get people prepared for change.

—make extensive efforts to get line-management buy-in on applications of corporate policy and practices. These efforts may include such devices as seeding well-prepared managers in distant organizational units.

—measure and monitor progress continually.

—evaluate the outcome—how do people feel about what has occurred? At IBM the corporate staff feels great about the employment-security practice; people in the field generally feel good about redeployment. The stage is set should the company need to make a major remissioning and redeployment effort again. Through the experience of the past two years, the company has not only achieved its business and personnel objectives, but has strengthened its capacity to execute its policies and practices in the future.

■ IBM is able to provide employment security to its employees because it has the necessary communication system; has a reward system to induce some line managers to nudge people to accept redeployment and other line managers to hire redeploys; and has a training system for people who have decided they want to change careers. Both commitment to full employment and the ability to execute top management's commitment have been brought into full development.

MUTUALITY VERSUS LEGISLATION

Chapter Nine

An Employee/Company Partnership   Full employment is the result of a partnership between a company and its employees. Without employees' willing cooperation a company would be hamstrung in attempting to provide full employment. Without this partnership no company, IBM included, could afford to offer full employment. It cannot be provided by a company unilaterally.

Employees, like the company, have an obligation to do their part to make full employment a reality. Mutuality makes the full-employment practice possible.

What are the obligations of the company, and what are those of the employees? The answer is not complex. The company's obligations are to plan carefully so that people have productive work to do and to provide retraining and relocation assistance to its employees when necessary. The obligations of the employees are to be reasonably flexible about relocation and reassignment and to accept redeployment as needed. When both sides meet their obligations, there exists the partnership which makes employment security possible.

Certainly the company is the senior partner by virtue of its breadth of view about the business situation and the magnitude of its resources. Hence the company must define for its employees how much flexibility is needed to make the business successful. It should inform people clearly as to the reasons for redeployment and provide enough opportunity and financial and personal support so that employees volunteer for redeployment.

On their part, employees need to take the company's needs seriously and be prepared to make short-term sacrifices and endure certain inconveniences. In the longer term, if the company is successful, redeploys are likely to have advanced their careers and feel better about themselves.

Our interviews with redeploys were replete

with statements of willingness to adapt to IBM's changing needs.

"My job at IBM has been a partnership," Carol Parillo from Westlake told us. "You have to show management you're willing to learn. You can do a lot of things on your own to prepare yourself for new jobs and opportunities. I was able to observe different things and then get interested in new jobs and prepare myself for them.

"Something like a major redeployment affects every single individual. Nobody comes out unscathed. People are usually prepared for something like that. People are upset. Most people can't make a decision right away. They need time. If the company tries to force people, it will lose in the long run. If an employee is happy with making the move, the company will win. If an employee is not happy, he or she should be helped because people come unglued. There need to be counselors; there needs to be patience; and management has to do its work with all the integrity they have."

"There is a bathtub effect," Walt Burdick, IBM's vice president of personnel, commented. "The most difficult time in the redeployment effort is when the company is going into it or getting out of it."

The reason for this involves the need to communicate with managers and employees about why the corporation is taking certain steps. When a redeployment initiative begins, all must know why the company is undertaking it and what their role is to be. When the initiative is ending, they must know why and what are the consequences for their own efforts.

"We've got to make sure," to paraphrase Burdick, "that the branch manager in one location has the same understanding of the business problem as the manager in another location. Those are the sender and receiver elements of a redeployment program, but the employee who is in the middle of all this also has to have an understanding of what the company is trying to accomplish. The points of transition in and out of a redeployment effort are crucial and difficult because of the extensive communications efforts required."

He added, "Then, especially, the company must have the support of all levels of its work force to make full employment possible. We must have their understanding and conviction, and to help achieve that we bring in the senior line executives to talk with them.

"The resource balancing accomplished in the last two years is an outstanding accomplishment," Burdick told an audience of IBMers. "It's the largest resource balancing achievement in our history and probably in the history of free enterprise. It wouldn't have been possible, however, were it not for the cooperative spirit and flexibility of our employees . . . employees who are willing to be retrained, redeployed, and, in many instances, relocated. It's an excellent example of a partnership at work. It gives me a great sense of pride, and it should give you that sense of pride, too. It also gives me great confidence, confidence that we could do it again should business conditions require . . . it gives me confidence that we're poised to participate in industry growth when it occurs, and it gives me great confidence that we can continue full employment on into the future."

How Employees Viewed the Redeployment/Relocation Experience
To the IBMers who experienced it, the redeployment/relocation experience was generally a favorable one. A survey of people who were redeployed showed that they were, on average, more favorably disposed than other IBMers to relocation and retraining. It is possible that this reflected an earlier bias in favor of relocation or retraining which caused people to select to be redeployed (virtually all redeployment was voluntary); but even if there was a predisposition, the experience did not turn them against it.

Despite IBMers having relocated and changed careers often, many were favorably disposed to relocation and retraining. In fact, IBM employees were more willing to relocate and/or retrain than the citizens of Boulder and Greencastle generally.

More than 90 percent of those relocated and those who changed jobs in the redeployment effort described the changes as voluntary. Those who relocated felt better about the move several months afterwards than they did initially. And four-fifths of the redeploys said they were willing to do so again if the company had need.

Yet it would be inaccurate to picture IBMers as simply sacrificing in order to help out the company. Though some inconvenience was undoubtedly involved for those who relocated, redeploys generally saw their career changes not as personal sacrifices but as career opportunities. Asked why they accepted a new position, 47 percent of the redeploys answered that it was a career opportunity, and an additional 29 percent cited their desire for diversity and challenge in their careers.

Asked about how the new position had worked out, three-quarters said that it had enhanced their careers. More than half rated satisfaction in their new careers higher than in the old. Sixty-one percent cited future career potential as higher in their new positions than in their old.

These are remarkable statistics. The setting was a business downturn. The company had a surplus of people in manufacturing and headquarters staffs. To meet difficult business conditions, the company had to move people about wholesale. An observer might have expected lives to have been disrupted and bitterness and insecurity engendered. People might have had advancement hopes crushed in downsizings and reorganizations as has happened in so many other American companies.

But there is no demoralization in IBM. There

is downsizing, but it is by retirements and normal attrition. Among those whose jobs are changed, instead of sacrifice, opportunity is discovered.

A business downturn is converted into personal career opportunity for thousands of IBM employees. That this was accomplished is perhaps the greatest accomplishment of the redeployment effort.

And the people recognized and appreciated it. In the downturn, they appreciated more the full-employment practice and the personal economic security it provided. They marveled at the company's capacity to give them new challenge and opportunity in the midst of its own adversity.

In a business downturn it might be understood that a company would draw upon the reserves of its employees' commitment and goodwill in order to persuade individuals to make sacrifices for the company. IBM did some, but very little, of this. Instead, in adversity it built its employees' commitment by making clear to them the security they had with the company, and astonishing them with the company's ability to provide opportunities for career advancement to them.

IBMers know about the full-employment practice. Of some 250 people responding to our survey, only one person professed ignorance of the practice. When asked how the practice affects their attitudes toward the company, 62 percent credited it with increasing their commitment (34 percent stressed the personal security it gave them).

Interestingly, people under forty-one were far less likely to express commitment to the corporation than older employees, permitting the speculation that commitment is an attribute of the older generation and far less so of baby boomers.

Finally, despite generally favorable experience with redeployment, IBMers did not hesitate to criticize the company's handling of the process. More than half said the company could have done better in its redeployment/relocation effort. Most (59 percent) insisted that procedures could be improved; others (25 percent) asked for more communications; some (11 percent) for improved training; and a few (5 percent) for better attention to the career disruption caused by spouse relocation.

How People Feel About the Redeployment Experience   It might be expected that IBMers with young children would be the least likely to look at a relocation favorably. Surprisingly, however, those with dependent children who were redeployed were more favorable about relocating than other persons in the company. They were also more satisfied with their new jobs than others.

As to the prospect of being relocated again, those with dependent children were more reluctant than others.

Minorities constituted a very committed group within the company. They were more likely than others to have joined IBM because of its employment practices; more likely to be motivated by recognition from peers or managers; more positive about relocation or retraining; more happy about their career change if redeployed; more pleased about the career enhancement of their new position; and more willing to be redeployed again.

Despite all this, they were more likely to have felt forced to make a position change, were less satisfied with their managers' assistance during redeployment, and were no more and no less critical of the company's management of the redeployment process than other employees.

Shorter tenure IBMers, those who had been with the company for less than two years, were much more likely to have been redeployed than others. They volunteered for relocation and retraining to a greater degree than others—perhaps because they were, on average, younger; perhaps because they were more anxious to please the company since they had been employees only a short time. They were less satisfied with their new position than other redeploys, and more critical of the company's management of the process. They were, by our measure, the least loyal of length-of-service groups; but in a company exhibiting very high commitment among all groups, this should probably not be overstressed.

Women and men expressed the same motivation profile and feelings about relocation. Women were somewhat more interested in retraining. A larger proportion of women than men were redeployed, and women accepted relocation and career changes more willingly than did men.

Women were somewhat more dissatisfied with their new positions than men, but nonetheless saw greater career potential in their new positions than men.

Managers exhibited a greater responsiveness to motivation by the recognition of their own managers and their peers than did rank and file IBMers. They were less positive on relocation, in part because they have moved so often; but despite personal reservations were more likely to volunteer for redeployment than others. They saw their careers enhanced by redeployment, but were less likely to volunteer again for it. They received less formal training for their new positions and were more critical of how the company managed redeployment than others.

The picture one receives of IBM managers from our interviews and surveys is of people who are loyal to the company and prepared to volunteer for whatever assignments or locations it requires, but who are personally tired of relocating and are critical of the way the company manages the process—even though they play a crucial role in it.

Perhaps it is not surprising that IBM managers seem to be ambivalent about redeployment. They have a dual role in it. They are both key actors in the process and its subjects. So they are critical of the process, despite their own deep involvement in it.

That IBMers and especially the managers among them are often critical of the way the redeployment process was handled should not be taken as solely a negative. Quite the contrary. All the hard evidence and most of the soft (i.e., opinions and attitudes) indicate that the process was a great success. People voluntarily changed positions and were relocated and retrained; and they are on the whole favorably disposed to the results of the process. So criticism from them cannot be treated as suggesting failure of the process.

On the contrary, criticism is evidence of the continuing search for excellence within IBM. Employees have no hesitation about saying that the process was effective and its results good, but that it can be improved. The expectations of both rank and file and managers are high as to how their company should conduct a redeployment program and how it should treat its employees. Shortfalls are not lightly tolerated, and people are ready to call attention to them.

Finally, in the 1985–87 effort, most redeploys were first apprised by their immediate managers of the job opportunity they eventually took. This fact speaks well for IBM managers. Ordinarily, supervisors are reluctant to part with good employees, since the performance of their units may be adversely affected. Yet IBM managers searched out eager and ambitious people who could successfully handle new careers and pointed them away from their existing jobs.

Asked why they did so, managers gave various answers. Some said that the company needed the people elsewhere and so they felt they should release those who wanted to go. Others said that their units were going to be reduced anyway so that there was no ability to hoard people regardless. Finally, others noted that the reception and surrender of people was a common cycle in the company, "the way the game is played," and that they relinquished good people in the expectation that at some later date they would receive good people into their own units. Because there is so much movement of managers in IBM, managers were satisfied to have good people well distributed in the company, presuming that as they moved they would encounter organizations staffed by good people.

What **A**mericans **T**hink **A**bout **L**ayoffs   What do Americans think about layoffs? Most view them as unfortunate but unavoidable. We asked residents of Boulder and Greencastle, both communities with recent experiences of layoffs or plant closings (layoffs by Storage Technology and other companies in Boulder, but not by IBM, and a plant closing by IBM in Greencastle), if they thought companies should lay off people in a business downturn. Seventy-one percent replied yes, many asking rhetorically, "What choice do they have?"

But IBMers do not agree. Instead, by a large majority they are of the view that IBM should not lay people off, and that neither should other companies. This was something of a surprise, both to me and to several IBM executives with whom I discussed the matter. Generally, we expected IBMers to say that IBM is a special case—that it should not lay people off, but that other companies may find themselves in positions in which they must let people go.

But the response was quite different. Neither IBM nor other companies should lay off, said IBMers. It was as if they have concluded that other companies could behave as IBM does if they had the will. Having experienced full employment, IBMers believe others ought to have it, too.

Women, minorities, and short-term employees felt most strongly that companies should not lay off, perhaps because they are the groups most likely to be let go if a layoff occurs. IBM managers were also very likely to believe there should not be layoffs. About 20 percent of IBM managers said IBM should lay people off; and almost half said other companies should, when business conditions warrant. Perhaps managers are more familiar with how difficult business circumstances can get; perhaps they are eager to use layoffs as an opportunity to dispose of poorer performing employees. Whatever the reason, they seem least supportive of the full-employment practice.

Looking for **Career Opportunity**   Companies today are highly dependent on their capacity to create new skills among employees. The ideal employee is one who has the capacity to perform very different types of tasks over his or her work life. The evidence from Europe is that many Europeans have this flexibility just as do many Americans. This is especially true of IBMers, because the company so often looks for this quality in the people it hires.

   European employees of IBM appeared to be no less interested in career changes than their American counterparts. People were admitted to training classes after successfully completing aptitude tests, but once in the classes performance seemed independent of age, educational level, and previous function. Adults with the necessary aptitude and personal motivation learned well, supported one another in the classes, and completed their training.

   In order for there to be a balance between supply and demand, the company must have done an adequate job of anticipating the direction of its business and must have buffered its work force sufficiently.

   This observation reminds us that redeployment is not an objective in itself, but instead is medicine which the company and its people must take to correct something that went wrong, such as failing to meet goals in the marketplace, or alternatively, failing to anticipate a downturn in the business early enough.

   The second limitation involves the capacity of people to adapt. There is much value to education, but there are nonetheless limits to the ability of individuals to move from lesser skill occupations to those requiring considerable technical expertise. And despite all the success stories about people who go into sales, formal training can give a person the knowledge but not necessarily the drive to become an effective salesperson.

A company must recognize the limits to redeployment and not exceed them.

Critical Success Factors in Redeployment   Georges Savy is administrateur directeur général of IBM Europe and one of the five members of the executive office committee. He identified the critical success factors of a redeployment effort.

First, demonstrate top management involvement. The responsibility cannot be delegated to a staff whose role is primarily to support the management team.

Second, create, through proper communication, an environment where employees will look at redeployment as an opportunity for new careers and new challenges.

Third, redeployment must be managed as a quality project in order not only to achieve the numbers but also, and even more important, to ensure that the redeployment meets both the business needs and the employees' expectations.

Will Legislation Undermine Mutuality?   Mutuality must be stressed because in their pursuit of high employment levels, governments sometimes enact laws intended to make it harder for companies to be relocated and/or lay off employees. It might seem that a company that doesn't lay off would not be affected by such laws, but unfortunately such legislation is likely to make it more difficult for companies like IBM to provide full employment.

Why is this? The answer lies in mutuality. Legislation threatens to knock out the basic underpinning of employment security because it threatens mutuality. By appearing to convert employment security from something an employee earns by adaptability and adjustment to change into a legal entitlement, legislation undermines the partnership. Legislation offers a false hope because it places all its burden on the company and none on the employees, as if a company acting without employee flexibility could provide the reality of full employment. Ordinarily, it cannot.

IBM is an especially significant company about which to consider the impact of possible legislation, because it is large enough to come close to being a microcosm of the American economy as a whole as it will appear in the future. It has both engineering and manufacturing elements, strong research and development, extensive sales forces, a major financial sector, distribution and trade, and wholesale and retail elements. Its population is distributed among blue-collar and white-collar occupations, among professional and nonprofessional jobs, and among men, women, and minorities, much as the American work force will be distributed in the 1990s.[1]

Specifically, in the spring of 1987, IBM had only 12 percent of its employee population in blue-collar jobs as opposed to 27 percent for the nation as a whole. In contrast, it had 47.5 percent of its people in managerial and professional occupations, as opposed to 25 percent for the nation, and 40.5 percent of its staff in technical, sales, and administrative positions, as opposed to 31 percent for the nation. Finally, the nation had 13.5 percent of its work force in personal service occupations, where IBM has virtually

---

[1] See D. Quinn Mills and Malcolm Lovell, "Competitiveness: The Labor Dimension," in Bruce R. Scott and George Lodge, eds., *Competitiveness and the American Economy* (Boston: Harvard Business School Press, 1985), pp. 429–54.

none. In the future, blue-collar occupations will decline in America toward the low IBM proportion, and professionals and technical persons will rise.[2]

In looking at mutuality and full employment in the IBM corporation, we obtain a vision of what is possible for the nation as a whole in the decade ahead. People will be more adaptable because they are better educated and have a more professional approach to their occupations. Hence it is reasonable for the nation to expect them to take responsibility for many of the adjustments necessary to make themselves competitive in the modern world. It is in consequence a serious and unnecessary mistake for legislation aimed at employment security to be predicated on actions by companies alone.

Provisions in existing or proposed legislation such as long advance notice of plant closings or remissionings, while well intended, deprive a company of flexibility and rapid movement. Consultation about decisions to close plants or redeploy people holds up to employees and community residents the often false hope that employment in particular jobs and at a particular place can be preserved without substantial adjustments to a changed economic situation. It is a false promise and one that undercuts mutuality—making the company and its employees not partners but antagonists.

Many European countries have had legislation that requires extensive consultation between management and employees before facilities can be closed, work moved, or people retrained. Ordinarily these laws do not directly prohibit layoffs but instead try through various processes to minimize them. These regulations make more lengthy and costly IBM's efforts to provide full employment in Europe. There is evidence that IBM's European em-

---

[2] Ibid.

ployees know this. In its employee surveys IBM asks the question, "How satisfied are you with your security that you will be able to work for IBM as long as you perform satisfactorily?" If laws in Europe that hinder layoffs had any significant effect, one might expect to find European IBMers responding with greater certainty of employment security than those persons employed by IBM in the United States, which until late 1987 had no such regulations. In 1986 IBM took a survey when the business downturn was deep in the United States and just beginning in Europe, so that Americans might be thought to have been especially fearful for their jobs. Yet American employees answered with the same overwhelming majority that they were satisfied with their employment security as did employees in France and Germany. The responses were similar for both managerial and nonmanagerial employees. These results occurred despite extensive legal requirements in France and Germany designed to support employment security.

All over the world IBM and its employees attempt to meet their obligations to each other. The partnership works. So long as this is true, government regulations intended to provide greater employment security actually add nothing. The IBM employee, protected in his or her employment by a partnership with the company, gains nothing from legislation.

Also, legislation tends to make it more difficult for the company to provide employment security. In Europe, regulations cause delay in taking actions needed for business reasons, and also add to costs. Legislation such as that proposed in America, though enacted to only a limited degree, would have the same result.

Further, there are so many national jurisdictions in Europe with different laws that it is difficult to adjust the balance of resources in a company to maintain full employment.

Should the various states in the United States enact legislation with differing provisions about plant closings and layoffs, then the situation in America could become even worse than in Europe. American companies, including IBM's American operations, are unfamiliar with the additional complexity of managing in a balkanized environment. If the states enact differing laws, as they now seem likely to do, it will become much more difficult for a company to make necessary adjustments to a changing business environment. This will make full employment much more difficult to realize.

Full employment is best served by a corporate commitment voluntarily entered into and made possible by a partnership with employees. Where such a corporate practice exists, legislation adds no value and may be pernicious— by increasing the company's costs, or worse, by undercutting mutuality.

However, the fact is that most American companies do not follow a practice of full employment. Instead, most companies lay off employees and often do it with so little notice that people cannot prepare in a reasonable way. Communities are continually being devastated by closings and layoffs with insufficient notice and little or no assistance from the company involved.

But abuses by many companies should not blind us to the fact that legislation is not the best response. The better solution by far would be to help companies realize that by proper planning and management, and through a partnership with their employees, layoffs can be avoided and the company's long-term business performance improved. Hence in a business downturn people would not get pink slips, but instead take vacations, retrain for other work, or relocate.

What full-employment companies ask, and what IBM's record of decades-long employment security entitles it to expect, is that a company's management team be protected in its ability to do what is right for the business, including closings and redeployments if necessary, when done in the context of the enlightened corporation's principles.

If legislation passes, it should exempt those companies which follow a legitimate full-employment practice. There is ample precedent for this approach in the legislation which exists in many states and localities concerning South African business activities of American corporations. Where companies followed a certain code of conduct, they were exempted from the requirements imposed on those which did not. The circumstances are very different in other respects between the South African issue and that of employment security in our own country. However, legislative recognition that companies which do not contribute to employment insecurity should not be treated as if they do, is a valuable and proper principle to be applied in any legislative approach to plant closings.

Summary

■ Maintaining full employment is a cooperative venture between a company and its employees. The company must plan and manage its activities so that violent fluctuations in staffing are avoided, and employees must be flexible about work assignment and location. Employer planning and employee flexibility are the foundations upon which employment security is based.

■ Proposed legislation about plant closings and other threats to job security fail to adequately consider the mutual nature of the obligations upon which it must be based. Too often, no obligation is placed upon employees to be adaptable in what is, after all, a rapidly changing world. IBM's experience shows that the employees of a company can be very flexible and can find personal satisfaction in new challenges.

■ Despite the company's experiencing a business downturn, IBMers saw personal career opportunity in the redeployment process. What could have been a depressing experience instead became exciting. Both the company and individual employees deserve the credit for this. It stands in stark contrast to the morgue-like atmosphere in many of our companies which have been under economic pressure in recent years. IBM did not just suffer during the downturn; nor did it allow the marketplace to impell it into actions which could demoralize its staff. Instead, corporate adversity was transmuted into individual opportunity by a management alchemy that leaves the company intact and stronger for the experience.

■ There is a strong commitment among IBMers to the corporation. The full-employment practice is cited as a major source of loyalty, and commitment is given expression in a willingness to retrain and relocate, even among employees who have already changed careers often and are tired of relocations.

■ IBMers have high expectations as to their company's conduct, and despite a very favorable redeployment experience, are not hesitant to say the company could have managed the process better.

■ IBM employees are far less willing than most Americans to accept as a fact of life, albeit unpleasant, that companies must lay off people in business slumps. Instead, IBMers believe that their own company need not lay off, nor others as well. Because IBM has full employment, and is able to do so because of careful planning, they believe other companies can do the same.

It is as if they have been to the top of the mountain and have glimpsed the promised land.

It is as if they have said, "Don't tell me about how things are, let me tell you about how they can be." This can occur, they seem to say, if only managers will take responsibility for the security of their employees, and ask their employees to assume their role in the partnership.

THE PAYOFF IS COMMITMENT

Chapter Ten

What does IBM get from the effort it puts into providing employment security for its employees? The company insists that its no-layoff practice makes good business sense. What basis does it have for this conviction, and is it accurate? Full employment costs IBM a substantial amount of money in the short term. Are the benefits worth the expense? Are IBM stockholders being short-changed by full employment?

Keys to High Employee Commitment   Successfully managing an organization is always the result of finding a proper balance between the needs of the company on the one hand and the aspirations and expectations of its people on the other. The difficulty of locating the proper balance is increased because both sides of the balance are continually changing.

Good managers are concerned with achieving the balance on an ongoing basis. They try to understand the motivation of people so that they may present the company's needs to them in such a way that the employees recognize in the company's needs opportunities for themselves. They try to understand the attitudes and expectations of employees so that they may build commitment to the company and its goals.

IBM's top management is convinced that work-force commitment contributes to its business success. In our interviews, executive after executive stressed that the company asked a very great deal of its employees in work effort, commitment, and flexibility, and that because of the intense loyalty of its employees, the contribution was forthcoming.

Because of this conviction, the company takes employee morale very seriously. Through internal opinion surveys it continually measures the attitudes of employees toward the company and attempts to determine what factors contribute to enhancing employee satisfaction and morale.

Other large companies also are concerned

about employee attitudes. A group of thirty-two of America's largest employers years ago established an organization for the sharing among themselves of data obtained from employee questionnaires. The companies include banks, manufacturers, natural resource firms, retailers, and insurance companies.

Each company surveys its own employees (or contracts out to a survey firm the administration of the questionnaire and data tabulation) but uses a group of identical questions. Many companies in the group employ hundreds of thousands of people, so some choose a random sample for the surveys. A company of IBM's size surveys four thousand people in the United States each year with these questions (this is in addition to its own ongoing survey program). A data processing agent serves as the consolidator of the data, preparing a report which shows the average response on each question which had a numerical answer. Each company that is a member of the group receives the pooled data and compares its own employee responses against those of the group of companies as a whole.

IBM belongs to this group of companies and carefully monitors its employees' responses against those of the other companies. On the items that together constitute a measure of employee morale, IBM stands well ahead of the pack and has seen its advantage grow substantially in recent years.

Beside the joint sample-based effort with other companies, IBM conducts regular surveys of all of its employees. The company's questionnaires use a core group of forty-six nonvarying inquiries, and additional questions may be added by operating units according to the circumstances at the time (the total number is usually between 80 and 120). Every employee in the company is included in this survey at least once every two years.

By combining a set of questions from the company's own survey, IBM creates a morale index. When the index drops, IBM executives study the reasons and the locations in which the drop has occurred, and takes remedial steps.

The process was initiated by IBM in 1956 when Richard Dunnington was hired from the faculty of the College of Business Administration at the University of Washington to find a way to help managers deal with people less by hunch and more by firm evidence about how employees felt about their work, their company, and how they were being managed.

In 1957 the opinion survey program was started in one IBM location, and has now spread worldwide. The effort includes not only the filling out of a questionnaire by employees and the tabulation and analysis of the responses, but also follow-up or feedback meetings with their colleagues and managers about concerns and corrective action.[1]

Not only are the dips and rises of employee satisfaction monitored at each division and location so that management action can be taken in specific instances, but since 1967, a company-wide morale index has been compiled. The index is examined in detail at least twice a year by the management committee at corporate headquarters. By the use of survey data, the company actively monitors morale on an ongoing basis.

Employment Security   Closely associated with the morale index is the issue of employment security. For many years IBM's strongest performance in the surveys, compared to the other companies, has been in the area of employment security. Al-

---

[1]   Harrison Kinney, "As You See It," *Think*, 1982, reprint available from IBM.

ready well above the average, even during IBM's business downturn, employees' positive feelings about job security continued near a record high, both in absolute terms and in comparison to employees at other companies. In 1986, in the midst of the downturn, IBM's employees gave the company a favorable rating on job security which exceeded the average in other companies by thirty-five out of one hundred points.

This was the morale opportunity which its business downturn presented to IBM. Rather than have a downturn result in layoffs and declining morale, IBM saw an opportunity to enhance its reputation with its employees, and thereby to build corporate loyalty. The company seized the opportunity.

In consequence, IBM passed through a major business downturn while simultaneously building its advantage over other companies in terms of the favorable attitudes of its employees toward the company. A short-term business reversal was made the occasion for strengthening a long-term business advantage.

During the downturn not only the company but also many of its employees saw opportunity. They applied for redeployment to advance their own learning, experience, and careers. The way the business was managed—with its reliance on redeployment and retraining—and the way people thought about their careers—with acceptance of challenge and change—reinforced each other. In a sense, the company thinks like the people, and the people think like the company. This constitutes a significant coincidence of approach and values which is an important element of corporate loyalty.

Repeatedly in our interviews employees pointed to the full-employment practice as a basis of their loyalty to the company. Dick Callahan, who retired from IBM at Greencastle, commented, "It cost IBM a lot of money to do what they did at Greencastle, but in the long run it's a money-maker to them. They've earned more loyalty. People do that extra little bit for you. I would have said yes and moved if the company had needed my help. It goes right down to the job and how one feels about the company. There's always a day of reckoning. In other companies there's not that much loyalty. Many employees are just there for a paycheck. I think IBM makes its money back."

Lynn Dorsett commented, "I really feel it's very unusual to be working for a company that can offer opportunity in career growth during some very serious and depressed business times . . . to get a new kind of experience that strengthens my hand in terms of my career. I think it is very fortunate . . . and very unusual."

Chris Polson was a manufacturing engineer at IBM's San Jose, California, plant who was reassigned to engineering in a test lab. "I was laid off once. The managers at that other company said to me, 'Here's two week's pay and you're out of here today.' " Then they hired me back and I noticed that the head person in quality control was very upset because the line was making garbage because the company couldn't train people fast enough to keep up with production. I went back after being laid off, but I didn't work as hard because I didn't trust people as much.

"Working at IBM I can build a foundation, then I can go to different areas and draw off that foundation. IBM doesn't hire from the outside except for entry-level positions and a few specialties. They will let me develop my career path."

Ted Tsutsui, formerly a senior design specialist who retrained to be a programmer, commented, "IBM is different from other companies because it cares about individuals and it also wants to look good to the rest of the world. If you treat somebody well, they'll work better. I worked at other companies before coming to IBM. IBM has treated me better. The environment is different."

Asked by us, not the company, about IBM's

full-employment practice, 36 percent of IBM employees in America (on a random sample basis) commented that it increased their loyalty to the company.

Such comments raise the issue of why so few other companies have a full-employment practice. In the mid-1980s I conducted a survey of the largest 250 companies in the United States and determined that fewer than .5 percent eschewed layoffs.[2] Most seemed to believe that there were no alternatives to layoffs. Yet the same companies were worried about employee morale and decline of corporate loyalty. The IBM experience indicates that whether a company has two hundred or two hundred thousand employees, morale and employee commitment can be much enhanced by providing employment security to employees.

Morale, satisfaction, loyalty, commitment, employment security, and work performance are not identical; but there is certainly a relationship. They are entangled in a web of reinforcing causality. While a company may be unable to separate them, or to measure the specific impact of each on the others, they are nonetheless mutually reinforcing. Employees talk about them interchangeably. But managers make distinctions. Increasingly managers do not look for loyalty, recognizing that many employees will not give it. "Loyalty is wearing the company's logo on your forehead," I have heard both managers and employees at other companies say derisively.

"It's outdated to expect loyalty," the chief executive of a large financial services company told me. "Employees have other alternatives than a single company, and we—the management—will lay people off whenever it will increase profits. We're not loyal to them; and they're not

---

[2]   D. Quinn Mills, "Planning With People in Mind," *Harvard Business Review*, 85, 4 (July–August 1985), pp. 97–105.

loyal to us. We have to find a way to manage without loyalty."

But there the difficulty begins. How does a company generate high morale and commitment when it has abandoned loyalty? And if morale and commitment lag, can performance be exceptional?

IBM insists that it has not tried to measure the impact of morale on performance, but it is clear that its executives believe the two are closely related.

"Full employment helps build satisfaction, morale, loyalty, and psychological well-being," George Krawiec said. "IBM is convinced that it is the right thing to do. We've had it for a long time. It is central to our principle of respect for the individual.

"We measure satisfaction and we measure morale," he continued. "We do not measure loyalty. It is too broad a concept, and too many factors affect it. And we have not made the attempt to tie morale and satisfaction, much less loyalty, directly to performance in a measurable way."

Many companies today have abandoned loyalty to their employees, and expect none from them. Certainly very few are willing to provide employment security. But these companies must nevertheless find some method of building employee morale and commitment or performance will suffer. A much-relied-upon method is to try to build morale and commitment with high compensation. This method, which has failed so spectacularly in American heavy manufacturing in the past several decades, as exampled by corporations with higher salary levels than competitors and lower commitment from employees, is now the strategy of many service-sector firms. In the long run, it is not likely to have greater success there than it has had in manufacturing.

Still, the employees of most companies are adjusted to the likelihood of layoffs. They do not pressure their companies to keep them. They say, as they did to us in our surveys of non-IBMers, "I got laid off but I adjusted; I found another job."

IBMers for the most part don't want another job. Ironically, one of the few IBMers we encountered who expressed bitterness with the company was an executive who had retired during the 1985–87 adjustment. "Full employment is for most of the people at IBM," he said, "but not for all. The company persuaded some of us to leave because it said it had to downsize and we believed it. So several of us retired. Now they are beginning to hire again, and we're hardly out of the company." This man is unhappy because he was persuaded to retire. He wanted to stay with the company.

At IBM employees want to stay with the company and want to do a good job for it. That is exactly what corporate loyalty, morale, and commitment are about.

Two-Way Communications   While very significant, employment security is not the sole key to corporate morale. Another major ingredient is communication between the manager and employee. The importance of communications was put in a provocative and challenging way by Jack Stillens, a recently retired IBM executive: "The true structure of an organization is the leader and the worker. The only reason middle managers are there is to be a communications link. This concept has gotten lost in American business today. Most companies have tried to build middle management ranks too strongly. Too many middle managers are trying to outguess the leader."

IBM has not lost sight of the role of the middle manager as a communications link. The significance of the connection between the manager-employee interface and employee loyalty to the company is best seen in the context of how the company manages generally.

IBM bases its corporate culture on three beliefs, one of which is respect for the individual.[3] In training sessions, IBM managers are shown how to apply the principles through specific policies, and in orientation sessions IBM employees are told to expect to be treated in accordance with the principle. So one of the elements of the opinion surveys which is closely monitored is what the responses say about respect for the individual.

Asked in the fall of 1986 about respect for the individual, employees identified privacy as the best example in terms of the manager-employee relationship. Asked about what respect for the individual means in terms of the company-employee relationship, employees identified employment security as the best example.

Results of the company's 1986 opinion survey also indicated a close correlation between respect for the individual and the quality of the two-way communication employees have with their immediate managers. That is, nonmanagement employees who report having very good two-way communications with their superiors also give the company a very favorable rating on living up to its principle of respect for the individual. But employees who report very unsatisfactory two-way communications with superiors also give the company unfavorable ratings on respect for the individual.

Employees sometimes complain that a manager fails to live up to the principle of respect for the individual when he or she plays corporate politics. Brad and Mary Geerdes relocated from Boca Raton, Florida, to Montvale, New Jersey, and thence to Somers, New York. "IBM is the best company to be working for," Brad told us, "because you never have to be concerned about being laid off. But one thing

---

[3]   Thomas J. Watson, Jr., *A Business and Its Beliefs: The Ideas That Helped Build IBM* (New York: McGraw-Hill, 1963).

that is disenchanting lately is that some of the managers I've worked for are out for themselves. They're worried about their own jobs and won't give me the freedom and flexibility to do mine."

Mary agreed, "People are less people-oriented because they're fighting for jobs. They're forgetting about respect for the individual."

"Yes," Brad added. "I put in the effort and some of my past managers wanted all the credit. I don't want to be treated that way."

What is remarkable is to hear improper managerial behavior, which happens in many companies, being objected to as a violation of a basic principle of the company. It indicates how strongly employees are attached to the IBM principles, how seriously they take them, and how quick they are to use them as a standard by which to judge their managers' behavior.

Two-way communication is also closely tied to the morale index itself. IBMers expect good two-way communication with their managers. Employees who indicated that they had poor two-way communications also gave their managers a very low rating. In fact, the difference in ratings given to managers by their subordinates differed by ninety-six points (on a scale of one hundred) between those who felt two-way communications were inadequate and those who found them excellent.

Even the employee's perception of the adequacy of his or her work load is closely tied to his or her perception of the quality of communications. Persons who registered poor communications also tended to feel that their work load was either too much or too little. Most of those who reported good communications felt that the work load was about right.

IBM's interest in communications is long-standing. In the late 1970s the company's opinion surveys told it that the more an employee knew about the company, the more favorably disposed he or she was toward it. So in 1981 the company launched a campaign to tell employees more about the company.

All of this is evidence of two basic factors which enhance morale. The first is the full-employment practice itself, because it is the item most often mentioned by IBMers as the best example of what respect for the individual means, and because it is so closely correlated with the morale index. The second is good two-way communication between manager and employee, because all aspects of good morale depend on this key communication link between the employee and the company.

These data results provide the empirical justification for the stress which IBM puts on its full employment practice and on the implementation of that practice through direct line management. The company tries continually to strengthen the manager-employee link, and makes this the focus of its corporate communications effort (as described in Chapter 9). Full employment, as evidence of the company's respect for each individual employee, combined with good two-way communications between manager and employee so that the employee knows what is happening, why, and what it means to him or her, are the keys to corporate loyalty at IBM.

Based on IBM's experience, what do other companies do wrong, or fail to do at all, so that the commitment of their employees leaves much to be desired? First, companies ask commitment from their employees, but do not give it in return. Once America had a work force which would give commitment without expecting anything in return. But those days are gone. Today's work force has the capacity for commitment, but feels that a company must earn devotion from its employees. IBM is prepared to earn its employees' loyalty by a variety of means that have been described in this book. All too often, other corporations are not willing to take the necessary steps.

Second, companies pick and choose among the elements of business culture, leaving out those which are crucial to building commitment. For example, in the past decade hundreds of corporations have embraced such principles as striving for excellence in all they do, keeping close to the customer, and putting quality first. But IBM adds to that list an equally important principle: respect for the individual employee. In literally hundreds of meetings with executives from other corporations in the past several years, I have been astounded at how readily top executives in many firms ignore this principle. Without a top-management commitment to the people in the company, middle managers ordinarily do not treat employees with the kind of respect which builds commitment in the rank and file.

Third, companies often fail to strengthen the key communications link between the first-level manager and the employee. Instead, in many companies communications are delegated to staff specialists, and first-level supervisors are intentionally or by default kept out of the communications effort. In some otherwise outstanding companies, top management so distrusts first-line supervision that it actively seeks to exclude them from communicating company policies to employees. This is an extreme situation, but it is common for companies to leave first-level managers very much in the dark about the company's situation and policies. If first-level management is to be brought into the communications link, a company must invest continually in training them for the role. Many companies prefer to avoid these costs. Hence, short-sighted cost minimization results in poor communications, and, through the chain of causation described above, poor employee morale.

Are the Stockholders Being Shortchanged? IBM's full-employment practice has recently had little support on Wall Street. Early in the research for this book I talked with several of the analysts who follow IBM closely, and though most asked me not to cite them by name, they generously shared their opinions about the company and its management practices.

In general, Wall Street currently perceives IBM's commitment to full employment as a mistake. This conclusion is reached despite analysts being aware of the advantages of the practice: that it builds loyalty, promotes retention of top performers (as well as, for that matter, other employees), and is a "classy thing to do," as one analyst put it.

In essence, the argument is that IBM has far too many employees for the size of its business and its expected growth rate (which they generally see as below that which the company experienced in the past). So full employment leaves the company stuck with many high-cost people, and the full-employment practice, by retaining them, constitutes an "atrocious management thing," to quote one analyst. Instead, the company ought to be downsizing far more energetically, and this requires extensive layoffs. "Mr. Watson wrote the Bible," said one analyst, "and it was right for its time. But it's right no longer. IBM's markets are no longer so secure. The company cannot afford paternalism. It must go to the greatest good for the greatest number, and that means layoffs."

Some suggested that IBM is able to follow its full-employment practice because it is so large that it is virtually immune from takeovers. The implication is that a raider would see employment security as an easy target. Asked about potential takeover attempts, Frank Metz, IBM's chief financial officer, commented that $90 billion (the market value of the company) would be a lot of junk-bond financing for a corporate raider to raise. He also pointed out that IBM is a highly integrated business which would be very hard to sell part of to raise cash after a successful takeover.

Metz described full employment as of "inestimable economic value" and added, "Make no mistake, I answer to the stockholders. If the business doesn't turn you'll be interviewing someone else."

Also, IBM's full-employment practice itself is probably a major barrier to a takeover. Litigation has been successful recently in enforcing the employment contract between a company and its employees, and IBM's contract arguably includes full employment. This would make downsizing the corporation or changing its management in large numbers very difficult or prohibitively expensive for a raider.

But though IBM may be largely isolated from what is currently referred to as the discipline of the capital markets, it is not protected from harsh criticism. One analyst put his view this way: "IBM has too many people. In the recent downturn of IBM's three constituencies—employees, customers, and stockholders—the stockholder has borne an unfairly disproportionate share of the burden. Layoffs would have permitted much more extensive cost reductions and given the stockholder a fairer return on his or her investment."

To such criticism IBM executives give several responses. Robert Oberholzer, a staff manager from headquarters who has recently accepted a position at Rolm in California, commented, "It's hard to get Wall Street to appreciate sufficiently the return to IBM on the full-employment practice. It's difficult to say how revenues will be increased to offset the company's expenses.

"But," he continued, "in terms of employee morale, we can place a value. Other Silicon Valley companies have a tremendous turnover. At IBM our turnover rate is in the single digits. We don't have the cost of the learning curve for new employees that other companies have as they keep hiring new people and bringing them up to speed."

"It's a matter of shared responsibility," Bob Gholson commented. "We tell our people that in good times we'll move them along in their careers. In bad times, we'll provide for you. As a result, everyone is in it together. It's not managers and employees, as it would be if we laid people off. Everybody is IBM."

Sherry Lambly said, "IBM has committed a great deal to the education and to the development of our people, and we simply don't want to lose them. The value in that is that we have the best-qualified people. We have high-quality individuals and there is loyalty and dedication as a result of our full-employment commitment."

Larry Coleman, at Indiana State University, has studied a number of companies with respect to their employment policies. "I say full employment is good management," he said.

Implicit in the critics' view is that IBM would have been better off in a business sense if it had laid off people rather than redeploying them. But IBMers insist that there is a real need for additional people in sales and sales support. The company now meets intense competition in the marketplace and many of its products are no longer so unique or of such high quality that they sell themselves. Instead, active sales efforts are needed to gain sales. IBM has also devoted little attention in the past to many smaller buyers, and now, with additional sales staff, will be able to go after those customers as well. And for the bigger customers, IBM will now be able to design systems to fit their specific needs on what is almost a partnership basis. The company intends to stress not only the performance of the hardware it sells, but software, documentation, training, a hotline for repairs, and maintenance.

Stephanie John commented, "In the past customers had things that they wanted to work with IBM on, and we didn't have the resource; we didn't have the people in marketing or systems engineering that we could apply to those projects." With the redeploys, the company is better able to work with its customers.

Many redeploys have brought technical skills from the factory floor to the sales office, and have strengthened the sales teams from this point of view.

Also, to a degree, the sales downturn which IBM experienced in 1985–87 was due to the company having lost touch with its customers. Top executives acknowledge an arrogance which blinded the company to the increasing exasperation of computer users with their inability to integrate hardware of different types and from different manufacturers. IBM's army of new salespersons will help the company avoid losing touch again.

Will the expanded sales force result in a substantial increase in sales in the short term? Possibly not, the company says, but the increased sales effort is a form of "investment marketing," to use an IBM term, which will pay handsome dividends in the future.

It is striking to contrast IBM's approach to a sales downturn with that of most other companies. Rather than react by laying people off to cut costs, IBM redeploys its work force into sales to build revenue for the future. Rather than downsize to wait for better times, the company increases its effort in the marketplace. IBM's actions demonstrate its confidence in the ability of its people to master the company's economic environment and to turn it to the company's advantage. It is a strategy of optimism and self-confidence in the face of adversity. Were the company to lose this feature, it would, as one executive said, "cease to be IBM."

In a sense, the full-employment practice drives IBM aggressively in the marketplace. Faced in a downturn with thousands of people for whom to find productive work, the company's managers scramble for business. Layoffs would make it much easier to be less aggressive, to wait for external events to bring a resumption in sales.

George Krawiec points out as well that layoffs are themselves expensive. In a seniority layoff, for example, the newest employees are released first. Recruiting and training investments are lost and then duplicated when new staff is hired in the upturn. Layoffs increase a company's unemployment insurance costs in states which do merit rating. Working relationships can be destroyed; quality of production and service declines; loyalty is lost; community relations are damaged. In any full costing of full employment these costs should be weighed against the direct labor cost savings from layoffs.

Given that there are some savings to IBM from the full-employment practice, what are the net costs of the practice? The company denies that it has a figure, and I have been unable to derive one. It is not that the company does not have many of the building blocks of an estimate. It does. For example, many of the costs of refurbishing Boulder for its remissioning were accounted for separately, so that estimates are available. But these are only partial costs, and full costs are very difficult to identify. IBM is continually transferring, relocating, and retraining employees. Much of what occurred as part of the 1985–87 redeployment effort would have occurred anyway. Netting out the ordinary from the exceptional would be an enormous task which has not been undertaken.

But costs may not be the real issue. IBM can afford the full-employment practice in its business environment today—in part because it is managed in ways that minimize the cost of full employment. So perhaps the proper question is not how much the practice costs IBM, but whether it has chosen wisely in spending money on full employment?

Ken Current, an IBM executive assigned to assist Greencastle after IBM closed its plant, responded to the question. "How can IBM afford to do the things we do? Because we've elected to. We work hard on economizing. Our corporate offices aren't lavish. We don't have private waiters to serve us lunch. Many executives don't have fancy automobiles. John Akers drives his own car to work. Extravagant things don't happen at IBM.

"That's the way we've been able to afford treating our people well and the communities well. We maintain leadership in technology. Our people fly coach, not first class. Success gives us resources, and we use them to contribute to our competitiveness."

Studying IBM and its full-employment practice causes one to conclude that IBM doesn't provide full employment because it has more money than it knows what to do with, or in order to shortchange its stockholders, but because it plans for full employment and so minimizes the cost, and because it is convinced that it obtains long-term benefits which outweigh any short-term costs.

In an important way, the full-employment practice and the employee commitment it engenders helps to cushion the company against business reverses, even those occasioned by its own errors. When companies respond to adversity by laying off people, they often damage morale and create insecurity and confusion to such a degree that the company ceases to perform well in the marketplace and the downturn is made worse than it would otherwise have been.

The stockholder is not short-changed because the company chose to invest funds in full employment rather than to attempt to raise earnings-per-share a bit during a business downturn by laying off employees. Full employment is not a frill at IBM, but an integral part of its way of doing business. Hence the payoff for the stockholder of the full-employment practice is imbedded in the success or failure of the company in the long run. If IBM continues to be a successful company in the future, then full employment has served the stockholder well. For full employment is one of the factors that give the company its soul.

WHAT THE FUTURE HOLDS

Chapter Eleven

IBM has partially negotiated the perils of its 1985–87 business downturn. It is turning its business around and has preserved full employment. What of the future? Does the company have the management depth and capability to resume its past growth? Are its skills of execution blunted after the downturn, or has it honed them in adversity? In downsizing its employee population to reduce costs was IBM's muscle cut, or is the leaner organization more effective? Does the company have the management depth to continue its commanding position in so many aspects of the computer industry? Does IBM remain a good investment?

*Has **IBM** **P**assed **I**ts **P**eak?*   In recent years many observers of IBM have commented that the computer industry has reached a certain level of maturity and that as a result the years of IBM's rapid growth have ended. The company is faulted by some investment analysts for building up staff and production capacity in the early 1980s in anticipation of growth which did not occur. The full-employment practice is said to be a relic of earlier times when the industry was not mature and the company could grow rapidly. Today circumstances are different, it is said, and the company must junk its past management practices and become more like other traditionally managed organizations.

IBM executives agree with their critics to a certain degree. They acknowledge that their industry is changing, but they insist that it still provides the setting for rapid growth and that their basic managerial practices are as valid as ever.

In 1974 Nancy Foy, in her book on IBM,[1]

---

[1]   Nancy Foy, *The Sun Never Sets on IBM* (New York: Morrow, 1974), pp. 191, 10, and 193 respectively.

reached the conclusion that "IBM faces . . . the more important and long-lasting problem . . .: learning to live in the no-growth environment." She also commented that "now, as the computer industry matures and manufacturing technology improves, getting rid of people is a primary problem."

Prophecy is hazardous, and Nancy Foy may be forgiven for having been, in light of what has happened since, quite wrong. In the thirteen years since she wrote, IBM has added $39 billion in annual revenue, $3 billion in profits, and 100,000 employees. Far from being in a no-growth position, the company has expanded rapidly.

Nancy Foy noted in her book that the company dissented from her opinion that it had plateaued and faced a stagnant future. "IBM itself," she wrote, "doesn't necessarily accept the inevitability of a no-growth situation."

Similarly, today, when careful students of the computer industry insist that it is matured and that IBM's days of rapid growth are over, the company's top executives disagree.

Long-service employees at IBM have seen the industry go through stages. At the conclusion of each stage there was concern that growth had ended. First the industry had to be invented. Then the technology was spread to new areas. Today the industry is becoming a pervasive element of modern economies. There is no clear reason why the stage of making the industry pervasive should generate any less growth for IBM than did the earlier stages.

"The power is in the chips," Frank Metz, Jr., commented, "to make the human interface with the computer much easier, and even pleasant." No longer are the customers of the computer companies simply other companies; today they are individuals as well. As the human interface improves, the technology will become pervasive.

Today the computer industry is not simply a new business made up of start-up companies with promising futures, it has become instead a major participator in economies around the world.

IBM itself is now of great importance, and not only because of its technology. It is a large employer in most countries. In the United States and the European Economic Community it is the largest single taxpayer. What happens to IBM matters to far more people than only its employees and customers.

IBM recognizes that its industry is in another stage and that it must do some things differently. It has invested heavily in making its manufacturing plants among the most automated and lowest cost in the world. It is revamping its product line to meet competition. It continues to make very large investments in technological development. It recognizes that greater volatility in its industry will cause its revenues and earnings to become more volatile.

Organizationally, IBM recognizes that it must become more flexible to adapt to a more rapidly changing business environment. To do so it is making a major effort to decentralize much operational decision-making by delegating it downward. Its careful hiring and continual management education have provided the company with a managerial work force whose depth and talent is unrivaled.

IBM is now conducting its business with well over 15,000 fewer people worldwide than two years ago. The full-employment practice has not meant that the work force cannot be reduced and costs cut substantially.

A further positive consequence of the redeployment effort of 1985–87 is that the company has preserved most of its reservoir of good people. It is fully positioned for an upturn with experienced personnel, and can avoid the costly delays and expenses of initial hiring and training of many people. Also, when companies lay off, they usually release the younger employees first, and in today's world these are the people who have the most up-to-date skills. By avoiding layoffs, IBM has retained its well-trained young people. Because the company is fully prepared to take advantage of the coming upturn, the business value of the full-employment practice may be demonstrated strongly in the near future.

The company's ability to execute its strategies and objectives is extremely strong, as the history of redeployment and remissioning recounted in this book demonstrates. The management structure of the company seems fluid and is continually being adapted to the specific business situation and to the individuals in top management positions. IBM seems irrevocably wedded to nothing in its business strategy or organizational structure, each of which will be changed as the business environment evolves.

The company has no plans, however, to alter its basic beliefs. If anything, pursuit of excellence and service to the customer seem more important now than before as the company confronts increasing competition.

Respect for the individual is also unlikely to be abandoned, but its key element, the full-employment practice, may become more difficult to continue. In the mid-1960s cutbacks in the space program made a number of IBM employees at Cape Canaveral surplus. Each one was offered a comparable job. In the early 1970s a recession hit the computer industry and over the next five years IBM retrained and redeployed thousands of people. The 1985–87 recession and consequent redeployment effort was the largest of all. With each of these experiences it seems that the difficulty and complexity of managing redeployments is becoming greater.

In part, this is because the company is larger and more complex. In part, it is because the suddenness and sharpness of the downturns is increasing. But whatever the causes, the trend to greater difficulty is clear. The future will be for IBM not only a test of its business acumen, but a test of its ability to continue the full-employment practice.

Hence, IBM is attempting to control more

closely its tendency to add people in times of good business. "Ten years ago," Gerry Marmion commented, "when we had problems, we'd throw more people in. . . . We've realized now that we can't throw people at the problem any more."

As the environment in which full employment is to be provided becomes more difficult, more is required of IBM's employees in the way of adaptability and flexibility. IBM is able to provide full employment by relying on its system of mutual obligation, and should employees become less rather than more flexible, full employment could be endangered.

Increasingly, IBM management sees itself in something broader than the computer business only. The company is a major player in the information industry generally, which includes computers, telephone, and satellites. Both investors and employees are more comfortable with IBM as the world's leading information company rather than a narrowly focused "computer" company. Also, the broader strategic definition of its business better serves a full-employment company than a corporate vision that is self-limiting.

Also, the company's staff will have to become more proficient in anticipating business changes and preparing for them. Yet it would be unfortunate if the effort to plan better adds to an already complex and resource-consuming process. The company needs to do not more planning in its current format, but better and more efficient planning.

The need for improved planning is occasioned by the more rapid shifts which the company is encountering in its markets, products, and external environment. Unless IBM can anticipate and prepare for these shifts, attempting to cope without layoffs will become too difficult.

Early in 1988, IBM reorganized to put all United States operations under a management unit which reported to the corporation's management committee. This decentralization was done in order to put operational decisions in the United States closer to the company's American customers and also to permit a more direct comparison of business growth and profitability among IBM's businesses in the United States, Europe, and Japan. IBM U.S.A. immediately began a further streamlining of American operations in order to make the company more competitive. The company is continuing to follow the managerial practices described in this book. In future facility remissionings and possible personnel redeployments, it should be anticipated that proposed courses of action will be submitted to the corporation's management committee for approval and that execution and monitoring will be done by the IBM United States organization.

Yet improved planning need not mean greater bureaucracy or expense. The planning process can be made more efficient and flexible. Probably the two—more effective planning and a more effective company—will go hand-in-hand at IBM.

The management style of IBM rests on three elements. The first is a faith-like commitment to the company's three principles of respect for the individual, the best customer service, and the pursuit of excellence, and the policies and practices by which they are implemented. The second is careful research of new products and their markets and the attitudes and behavior of the employees. The third is hard-headed business action, whether involving the introduction of new products, the closing of a plant, or the moving of an entire unit of the organization.

Although IBM's particular practices are not right for every company, these three basic elements of management apply across the board to every business. Every well-managed company must develop its own version of each. This is why IBM continues to provide such valuable lessons to persons interested in management.

Analysts of the information industry and IBM's executives have both pointed out that IBM now lacks the monopoly positions it once held, and as a result must compete harder and be better managed in the future. But critics of the company and IBM's top executives differ on what the implication is of this new fact of the company's life. Critics of the company suggest that the company ought to drop the full-employment practice. IBM's top executives come to the opposite conclusion.

"If IBM has a monopoly," John Akers told a Harvard audience in May 1987, "it is the way it manages its people." Referring directly to the full-employment practice, he said that in the long run the practice enables IBM to attract and hold very fine people. With this kind of top-management recognition of the company's long-term best interest, the prospects for IBM's future seem bright.